THE
GREAT WESTERN
RAILWAY
IN THE
1930s

ISBN 1870754 24 7
Printed by: Amadeus Press Ltd., Huddersfield
© NRM, D. Fraser, D. Geen, B. Scott
First Published 1985, reprinted 1992

THE GREAT WESTERN RAILWAY IN THE 1930s

VOLUME ONE

Compiled by
David Fraser • David Geen • Barry Scott

From the collection of
Mr. G.H. Soole

Runpast Publishing
10 Kingscote Grove, Cheltenham, Glos, GL51 6JX

Introduction

We hope that this collection of photographs will appeal not only to those who are students of the Great Western Railway, but also to those who are interested in railways in general.

The Soole Collection is held in the National Railway Museum at York, and was seen by us during our frequent visits. Discussions about the collection were followed by our being invited to fully annotate each individual print. During this work, it seemed to us that a publication using these photographs would be of great interest.

Although a few of the photographs have been published before, this is the first time that a complete book of Mr. Soole's work has been compiled. Further photographs of the Great Western Railway exist in the collection and a selection of these will appear in volume two.

Our own interest in the Great Western Railway started in railway modelling. The desire to produce more accurate models initiated our search for authentic information. Although all aspects of the Great Western Railway are of interest to us, our main area of research is the carriage stock.

The mid-thirties period of these photographs was one of change and this is seen in the various types of carriages featured. The demise of the Dean clerestory-roofed carriage was followed by the demotion of the Churchward designs as they in turn gave way to the standard series of Collett carriages which were found more and more on the main expresses.

The Great Western Railway Company's wagon stock was well established by the early part of the century. The few changes that occurred afterwards, were generally a modernisation of the existing range. Locomotive design reached its peak with the 'King' class of 4—6—0 in 1927 and thereafter only derivatives or specialised types were constructed to supplement the increasing numbers of 'Castles' and 'Halls'.

We have endeavoured to give as full a caption as possible highlighting the various points of merit and choosing a selection of photographs which probably gives a hitherto unparalleled view of the Great Western Railway in its heyday. In the appendix, we give details of the locomotives, coaching stock types and the train formations. The only important omission is the actual dates, these unfortunately were not recorded. Where possible, however, we have given a date which has been decided by either photographic evidence or by their position in the collection.

Godfrey Hewitt Soole was born in June 1913, the son of a vicar. He attended Huddersfield Grammar School then went to St. Catherine's College, Cambridge, where he gained his BA in 1935.

He joined the Great Western Railway in 1938 and was accepted, after gaining his MA in 1939, for the special training scheme. After service in the army during World War Two, he was demobbed in 1946 and rejoined the railway, continuing in service until he died suddenly while in office as Assistant to the Divisional Superintendent at Bristol in 1970. In 1960 he married the secretary of the Traffic Superintendent.

His railway photography started in approximately 1933 and in addition to his photographs of the GWR, he took many in the Cambridge area and during his trips to Canada in 1934 and 1936.

He was a member of the Cambridge University Railway Society and was one of the founders, in the mid-thirties, of the Bristol Railway Circle, of which he became a vice-president.

The photographs up to the mid-thirties were taken on quarter plate glass negatives and those up to the start of the war on 4½" x 3½" glass plates. His collection is now held for the nation in the archive of the National Railway Museum at York.

Apart from his interest in railways and photography he was also a keen climber, spending time in both Scotland and the Lake District pursuing this hobby.

Foreword

It gives me considerable pleasure to introduce this book devoted to the work of the late Mr. G. H. Soole. His was one of the first of several private photographic collections acquired by the NRM after its opening in 1975 and this is the very first book wholly devoted to but one of them.

Mr. Soole himself was probably concentrating on the locomotive aspect of the pictures he took but he recorded, quite incidentally, much other detail and atmosphere when it must have seemed that both the steam locomotive in general and the GWR in particular were permanent features of the landscape.

It is these incidental details, in particular the train formations to be observed behind the locomotive tenders, which first aroused the interest of the authors of this book. Since then, they have probably used the NRM library facilities to a greater extent than anyone else. It is therefore pleasing that the outcome of their researches serves both as a record of a fine, but little known photographer and as a detailed interpretation of one aspect of his work which, with the passage of time, has taken on a far greater value than Mr. Soole could, perhaps, ever have imagined when he first took the pictures.

J. A. Coiley
The Keeper,
National Railway Museum, York

This is the photograph which started off this work. We saw it on a desk in the library at the National Railway Museum at York. We looked at it and we were hooked. No. 6009 *King Charles II* stands in Brunel's old station at Bristol with a return working to Swindon. The local Swindon-Bristol trains were used to run-in locomotives fresh from overhaul. It gave a run of reasonable length which could be completed during the day and allowed an intermediate check at Bristol. The visible portion of the train on this day is a 'B' set comprising brake-composites of diagram E140. Note the reflections in the immaculate paintwork of the boiler, although by the marks on the smoke-box the locomotive has been priming slightly. Behind No. 6009 stands Bristol East signal box which was closed in November 1935. It is a beautiful building in keeping with this marvellous station; the ornate gas lamp bracket matching the style.

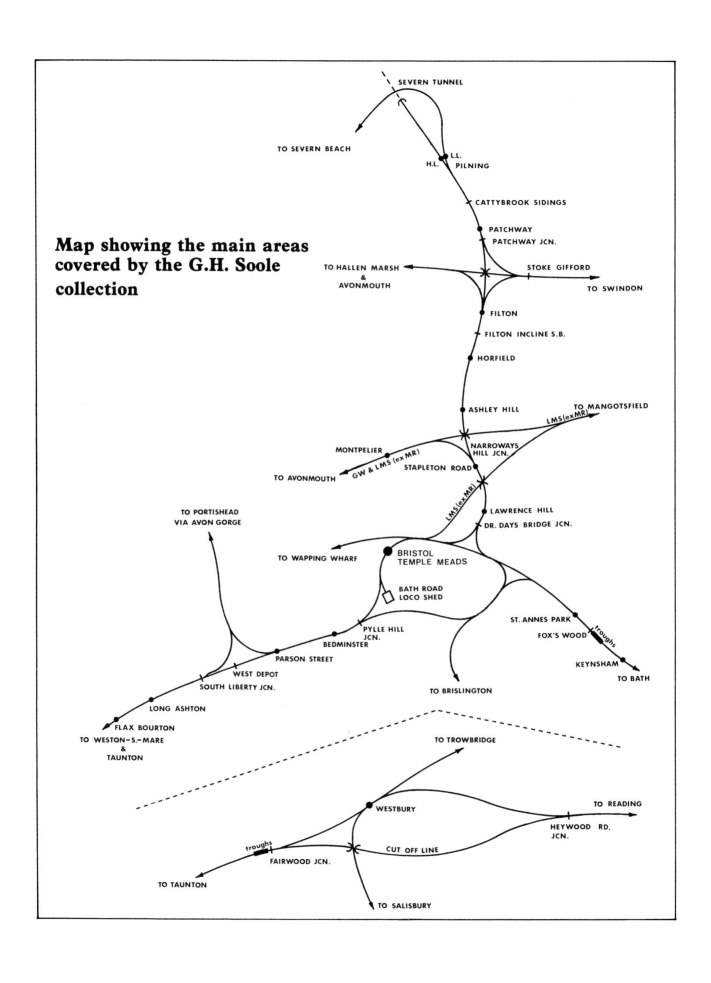

Map showing the main areas covered by the G.H. Soole collection

SEVERN TUNNEL

TO SEVERN BEACH

H.L.   L.L.
PILNING

CATTYBROOK SIDINGS

PATCHWAY
PATCHWAY JCN.

TO HALLEN MARSH
& AVONMOUTH

STOKE GIFFORD

TO SWINDON

FILTON

FILTON INCLINE S.B.

HORFIELD

ASHLEY HILL

TO MANGOTSFIELD

LMS(exMR)

MONTPELIER

NARROWAYS
HILL JCN.

GW & LMS (exMR)   STAPLETON ROAD

TO AVONMOUTH

LMS(exMR)

LAWRENCE HILL

DR. DAYS BRIDGE JCN.

TO PORTISHEAD
VIA AVON GORGE

TO WAPPING WHARF

BRISTOL
TEMPLE MEADS

BATH ROAD
LOCO SHED

ST. ANNES PARK

FOX'S WOOD

troughs

PYLLE HILL
JCN.

BEDMINSTER

PARSON STREET

KEYNSHAM

TO BATH

WEST DEPOT

SOUTH LIBERTY JCN.

TO BRISLINGTON

LONG ASHTON

FLAX BOURTON

TO WESTON-S.-MARE
&
TAUNTON

TO TROWBRIDGE

WESTBURY

TO READING

HEYWOOD RD.
JCN.

troughs

CUT OFF LINE

FAIRWOOD JCN.

TO TAUNTON

TO SALISBURY

1. Part of Bristol's redevelopment work is almost complete, new signals are installed and only debris needs clearing in this photograph taken from Parsons Street Junction signal box. The remains of its predecessor Portishead Junction signal box lies in the bottom left hand corner. 'Hall' class 4—6—0 No. 4987 *Brockley Hall* is about to pass at the head of a west to north express of LMS stock. Beyond, on the rear goods line, are vehicles of the four major companies.

2. An 'up' local train photographed at Bath station. The locomotive was presumably on a running-in turn from Swindon as No. 6016 *King Edward V* appears to be in an outshopped condition. One of the coaches in the train is worthy of note; the third one is the unique vehicle, to diagram D48. This was a 70′ 'toplight' brake third with three compartments and was No. 2366. The shabby signal box stands above the station buildings giving an overall view of the cramped station which was sandwiched between two bridges.

3. We see Maidenhead station with the third 'Castle' class locomotive to be built, No. 4075 *Cardiff Castle*. When constructed in 1924, No. 4075 was equipped with a 3500 gallon tender but by the time of the photograph it had been replaced with the 4000 gallon type. It will also be noted that the top lamp iron has been moved from the top of the smokebox. The open carriage truck behind the locomotive is a Scorpion 'B' or 'D' and is carrying a horse-drawn pantechnicon. Other items of interest in the photograph are the ATC ramp on the extreme left, the No. 2 cast iron lamp column with full harp suspension and what appears to be a capuchon on the safety valve cover of the engine.

Opposite page top:
4. The nameboards read 'Paddington-Bristol' on this 'up' express as it leaves Temple Meads. At the head of the train is No. 4061 *Glastonbury Abbey*, a 'Star' class locomotive built in May 1922. No. 4061 was the second to last 'Star' to be withdrawn after 35 years of service. The first carriage on the train is one of the 'Riviera' coaches built in September 1929 on Lot 1427 to diagram D105. Some of the debris from the government sponsored rebuilding lies near the signals while an LMS coach can be seen standing at Platform 12.

Opposite page bottom:
5. Bristol Temple Meads station with 'Castle' class No. 5048 *Cranbrook Castle* moving slowly forward on the 'up' middle road between platforms 7 and 9. No. 5048 was completed in 1936 and only carried the name shown here for sixteen months when it was renamed *Earl of Devon*. At this period it was shedded at Bristol Bath Road Shed. It is possible that the locomotive is moving forward to couple onto the train of LMS stock seen standing at Platform 9. The coach, No. 1936, which is visible on the right, was of LMS diagram 1899, and was built on their Lot 896 in 1936.

6. A track repair gang take a few moments respite to watch an 'up' South Wales express climb the last few yards to the summit at Patchway. Hauled by No. 5046 *Clifford Castle*, which is almost new, having been completed in April 1936, the train is made-up of thirteen coaches, about 400 tons, well within the permitted 455 tons allowed for 'Castles'. Among the carriages are several recently built and one very new vehicle, whilst the second coach has had a repaint of late. Not watching the express are two men who are more intent on collecting daffodils to take home!

7. An 'up' goods train climbs from Patchway Tunnel towards the station which can be seen in the top right. The banking engine and tunnel van (diagram AA4) will be detached at Patchway station and will use the cross-over seen to the right of the telegraph post to return on the other line to await the next train. A tunnel brake van was used in addition to the train van to provide extra brake power for the descent into the Severn Tunnel, each guard being required to stand by his hand brake. The guard in the tunnel van appears to be breaking the rules, which stated that side lamps should not be carried between Pilning and Patchway. They should have been fitted at Patchway station for the return journey. No. 2 banking engine on this day was '3150' class 2—6—2T No. 3176. In 1935 sixteen of this class were allocated to Severn Tunnel Junction shed for banking duties between there and Patchway.

8. A scene familiar to thousands of travellers along the A38 through the years was the advert for Bristol Zoo on the end wall of these houses. Not so familiar was the view below the road bridge. Easing down towards Patchway Tunnel is No. 5212 2—8—0T, a type which was used mainly in South Wales. Its train appears to be an empty coal train working back to the coalfield. This locomotive was one of the first batch to be built with outside steampipes. Of interest are the top feed pipes, which, on most if not all GW tank engines with sidetanks, ran along the tank tops to the cab, until modified to run through the tanks in early BR days.

9. 'King' class No. 6002 *King William IV* at the head of an 'up' express taking on water from Fox's Wood troughs. (Note water is coming out of the open filler seen above the locomotive cab.) On the left of the photograph can be seen the water tank which supplied the troughs. The pulley wheel on the side is for the float and indicator of water level, which here shows the tank is full. The track has reinforcement added to the ballast in the form of slabs to prevent it being damaged by the downwash. Covers for the two-track drains between the tracks are made from old Barlow rail.

10. A delightful photograph of a 'Dean Goods' 0−6−0 engine near Long Ashton, with a train from Bristol to the Cheddar line. These superb locomotives worked all over the system, performing all manner of duties. Here No. 2526 heads a local train, composed of a 'B'-set, towards Yatton where it will take the line to Wells. The local, or 'B' headcode, was normally carried in the upper position above the smokebox. The Bristol area used the lower position seen here. (This was normally the light engine, or 'G' headcode.) The 'B'-set coaches are of diagram E147 which, along with other contemporary vehicles, had only one door with a droplight in each of the double doors. A 'Bristol Division Train No. —' inscription can be seen on the leading end and would be repeated on the trailing end.

11. A 'Star' class 4—6—0 lifts a train up the main line past Narroways Hill Junction towards Ashley Hill. The line climbs from Stapleton Road station (which can be seen in the distance to the right of the church) for over three miles to Filton Jcn. From the right the lines come from Avonmouth, whilst those to the left above the locomotive serve the local gasworks, on which stands a rake of 'Eveson' and one 'Portwell Colt & Co.' wagons. The signal on the right would appear to be double-sided, but as the shadows show, is in fact two separate signals. In the right foreground is a catchpoint with emergency telephone and an ATC ramp is just beyond on the 'up' relief line.

12. A Swindon to Bristol stopping train drifts down the hill and around the curve from Ashley Hill towards Narroways Hill Junction. The train is headed by 4—6—0 *King Henry III*, which is on a running-in turn from Swindon Works after overhaul. The coaches are all Dean types, some in very good condition. The third and fourth vehicles are 6-wheeled saloons of diagram G20. These vehicles were built for family use, being allocated to different centres. Wealthier people could hire them and have the coach attached to a train to wherever they wished. After the Great War, this traffic dwindled and the coaches were used for other duties, some ending their days in the Traffic Department. It is possible to see the work carried out when this section of track was quadrupled in 1932/3. A totally new concrete footbridge has been erected as has a new rail overbridge which carries the LMS line. The brickwork on the left of both bridges is the original. Above the rail-bridge is the Muller Orphanage.

13. The 'up' Bristolian express is hauled by 'King' class 4—6—0 No. 6029, which was renamed *King Edward VIII* in May 1936, being originally named *King Stephen.* This was the last engine of the class, being completed in August 1930 and was shedded at Old Oak Common at this period. A nice uniform rake of 1936 stock is allocated for this train, most of the vehicles still showing evidence of the white roofs which soon changed to grey. The photograph was taken on the climb from Stapleton Road towards Filton, just after the train had passed Narroways Hill Junction.

14. A deceptive low-angle photograph, which hides the fact that 'Star' class 4—6—0 No. 4064 *Reading Abbey* is heading an express up the incline from Stapleton Road to Filton Junction. It is seen here rounding the curve from Narroways Hill Junction to Ashley Hill. *Reading Abbey* was one of the last batch of 'Stars' to be built in 1922 and was rebuilt in 1937 as a 'Castle' class.

15. A Bristol-Portishead local emerges from Clifton Bridge No. 2 tunnel with Brunel's Clifton Suspension Bridge in the background. The locomotive is No. 5565 of the '4575' class of small prairie 2—6—2T, and was built in January 1929, one of the last batch of 175 similar engines. These engines were found in most parts of the GW system, being used on local passenger and freight duties. The first two coaches are a Bristol Division 'B'-set to either diagram E140 or E145, the only difference being the bogie wheelbase. Note how well-kept the trackwork is, a credit to its gang. On the far side of the River Avon runs the A4 road known as Portway at this point. The freedom from traffic compared to today is worthy of note.

18. The sun shines from a stormy sky on 2–6–0 No. 4354 as it passes a freight train in the goods loop at Flax Bourton. No. 4354 is on its way towards Bristol with empty coaching stock. The third coach would appear to be in rather poor condition and may be on its way to Swindon for overhaul. The smoke from the engine shows up the bracket signal. This signal is rather unusual on plain trackwork and has been placed there to afford drivers a clear view. It also has a sighting board which was to assist visibility against the overbridge in the background. On the right can be seen two GW vans. The one on the left is a 'Mink C' of diagram V7, while that on the right, No. 114191, is a 'Mink A' of diagram V21 built on Lot 999.

Opposite page top:
16. A Temple Meads bound local train passes Stapleton Road signal box as it approaches the station of the same name, where it will call. The train has just turned onto the 'down' slow line from the Avonmouth branch which diverges to the left in the background, just discernible in the mist. This section of track, from Narroways Junction to Dr. Day's Junction, near Temple Meads, was quadrupled as early as 1891. This was to permit the through South Wales expresses a clear road without the congestion of local services. This was eased a great deal by the opening of the Badminton direct line in 1903, enabling the Welsh trains to by-pass Bristol altogether. However, it was still necessary to quadruple the rest of the line as far as Filton Junction in 1933. The train, an evening service, hauled by small prairie No. 5554, is of corridor stock. It is possible to see four differing styles of coaches here, Dean clerestory, Churchward's 'toplight' and Collett's early and later designs. Of interest are the various features, signal, telegraph post, point rodding, etc., as well as the large, three storey signal box. Today, the M32 motorway passes under the railway at about this same spot.

Opposite page bottom:
17. The driver and guard both watch Mr. Soole record this lovely portrait. Passing near Somerton, a '54XX' class 0–6–0 pannier tank is sandwiched between its two coaches, the task that these locomotives were designed to do. The leading vehicle is No. 213. Originally built in 1908 as 70′ steam rail motor No. 96, to diagram R, it was altered as seen here to an auto-trailer of diagram A26, in May 1935. Of note are the large oval buffers, gong and folding steps so typical of these vehicles. The bogies are of the 9′ American type. Immediately to the right of the front coupling is the connection for the auto equipment, enabling a similar coach to be attached in front. The linkage passes under the carriage to the locomotive. The fireman remained on the footplate to look after the engine while the driver was in the front trailer.

19. A 'County Tank' stands on the centre road at Reading. These 4—4—2T engines derived from the 'County' class 4—4—0, didn't last very long. They were displaced by the large prairie 2—6—2T engines of the '61XX' class introduced in the early '30s. All were gone by 1935, except for this engine No. 2243 which, although withdrawn in December 1934, lasted almost five years longer at Old Oak Common as a stationary boiler until August 1939 when it was taken to Swindon and cut up. The first four coaches are a London District 'D'-set comprising a close-coupled set, in this case of 'toplights', made-up of BK3rd, 3rd, 3rd, BK3rd. Notice the apparent use of every available space to hang advertisements, which must have provided the railway with a useful source of income. Of course at least two of these are GWR adverts, one of which is for Wales.

20. This photograph shows Haverfordwest station in what was Pembrokeshire in West Wales. No. 6339 heads an 'up' express from Neyland into the station in the evening, with a clerestory post office van (diagram L9) behind the tender. The chap in the blazer with a tennis racket amongst his luggage, is perhaps going to college or university and his family are seeing him off. Other features in the photograph are worthy of note namely, ornate gas lamps, poster notice boards, loading gauge over the end loading dock, with boards to assist loading lying on the ground.

21. The fireman of 'Castle' class No. 5022 *Wigmore Castle* watches Mr. Soole photograph his 'down' express. The train is standing at Platform 3 of Temple Meads, although technically the locomotive and first three coaches are also in Platform 4 because it is standing past the scissor crossover which separated the two. It would appear that the coach headboards have the blank side displayed. Note the advert for Dr. Barnado's Homes in the centre of the three on the wall below 'Bristol' and a GW notice exhorting passengers to 'Send your luggage in advance' on the left.

22. Two workmen glance at No. 6024 *King Edward I* as it enters Platform 10 at Bristol Temple Meads with an 'up' express. Colour light signals and electric point motors show that the rebuilding is almost complete. Only some finishing off is required at the platform ends. The platform on the left was the best place for train spotting because as well as watching the comings and goings, a sharp pair of eyes could see what was 'on shed'. Note the two open wagons being used in the reconstruction just to the left of the locomotive.

23. 'Castle' class No. 4094 *Dynevor Castle* stands at Platform 9 at Bristol Temple Meads with its 'up' express awaiting departure time for London. There is still evidence of the reconstruction taking place in the form of the fence around the East signal box, the new platform and the new colour light signal gantry. Two small prairie tank engines can be seen on the right standing in the terminus station which was used for local services.

24. 'King' class 4—6—0 No. 6029 *King Stephen* eases under Bath Road bridge and past the engine shed into Platform 10 of Bristol Temple Meads. No. 6029 was renamed *King Edward VIII* in May 1936, after the death of George V. The train is running under a local 'B' headcode and has probably come from Weston-Super-Mare but will carry an express 'A' code for the onward journey from Bristol to London. On shed, where the clock shows 3.05 p.m., are two engineering department coaches, the left a former 40' PBV of diagram K4, the right a brake third 6-wheeled vehicle, originally of diagram T38.

25. A wintry sun shines down on a recently built member of the 'Castle' class, No. 5043 *Barbury Castle*, as it storms towards the summit at Patchway with an 'up' express. This photograph can be dated to early 1936, as No. 5043 was completed in March of that year and the first coach was altered in June. The locomotive was in fact renamed *Earl of Mount Edgcumbe* in the following year. As mentioned earlier, the leading coach can be identified and dated. It is either No. 2355 or No. 2365 which were to diagrams H17 and H18 respectively and were altered from brake thirds of diagrams D47 and D46 by the fitting of a buffet. This was removed in June 1936. The roof vent is still in place in this photograph just behind the leading toilet tank cover. The 'down' freight on the left is probably stopped while the guard pins down the brakes. It is composed of private owner coal wagons, some of which have end numbers visible. To the right an 'up' freight waits in the 'up' refuge siding which, judging by the owners' wagons, is bound for London.

26. A 'Saint' class 4—6—0 passes through Filton Junction station with a 'down' South Wales to Bristol local. Built in May 1912, No. 2949 *Stanford Court* has recently had new cylinders with outside steampipes fitted at Swindon. It also has a 3500 gallon Collett-style tender with continuous coal fender. The fine array of square wooden-post signals controlling the junction provide an excellent guide to the layout. The set in the centre control the 'down' relief (home and distant) with the lower bracket indicating a connection across to the 'down' main. The bracket signal on the right controls the 'down'-main-to-relief, whilst the taller home and distant control the main line. Behind the train can be seen the signals controlling the junction to Hallen Marsh and Avonmouth. Note also the ATC ramp in front of No. 2949.

Opposite page top:

27. '57XX' class 0—6—0PT No. 3731 working in the 'up' side of Stoke Gifford yard, shunting and assembling trains. This engine was very new when photographed here, being completed in July 1937. It was one of the 'modernised' design which had the improved cab with larger front and rear windows and a higher roof. The shunters truck, branded 'Bristol (East Depot)', is No. 41867, which was originally built to diagram M1. The box on the top contained tools, re-railing ramps and flags etc. Note that the 'W' irons are plated over. This was to prevent the shunters' toes or poles getting caught in the wheelspokes. The centre-spindle shunting signal on the left-hand signal post is of interest.

Opposite page bottom:

28. Photographed at the east end of Stoke Gifford yard on the goods line, is No. 2812 of the '28XX' class of heavy goods locomotive. This, the thirteenth locomotive of the class, was completed in November 1905 and was originally fitted with a half coned boiler. In 1910 the boiler was replaced by a fully coned type as in the photograph, but then the engine alternated between the two types for a further three changes of boiler until the fully coned type was standardised. The engine received outside steam pipes in 1947 when new cylinders were fitted, although the boiler in the picture was already able to take them. Behind the engine is a private siding with gate and notice and note also the beautiful yard gas lamp.

29. 'Star' class No. 4061 *Glastonbury Abbey* works a Plymouth to Wolverhampton express up towards Ashley Hill. No. 4061 has steam to spare at this point in the 3-mile climb from Stapleton Road to Filton. It will then head for the north to west route via the Severn Tunnel. The train is made-up of a mixture of stock, the leading vehicle being an ex-LBSCR 6-wheel milk van, followed by a variety of LMS and GWR passenger coaches.

30. 'King' class 4—6—0 No. 6014 *King Henry VII* lays a smokescreen over the Somerset countryside as she hurries a 'down' express over the Frome avoiding line. One 'King' class and one 'Castle' (*Manorbier Castle*) were streamlined in 1935, in an attempt to reduce wind resistance, but the experiment wasn't considered successful enough to develop further. By the time this photograph was taken some of the less practical panels had been removed to prevent overheating and to ease maintenance.

31. This photograph shows 4—6—0 No. 4098 *Kidwelly Castle* at the head of a 'down' express near Long Ashton. At this time No. 4098 was shedded at Exeter so will probably come off there or at Newton Abbot. The train may be the 'down' Devonian. The painted lining on the cab front shows up very well in this photograph. It will also be noted that this locomotive has not yet received a fire-iron tunnel. These were introduced from No. 5013 onwards in 1932.

32. A Cardiff-Brighton express passes the quarry at Fox's Wood and starts over the water troughs. The locomotive, 'Star' class 4—6—0 No. 4055 *Princess Sophia* fitted with an intermediate tender, heads south with two GW and three SR coaches. The GW locomotive will be replaced by a Southern Railway one at Salisbury. Fox's Wood signal box, which can be seen in the distance, controls the tracks into the quarry and the transfer line. Note how the end of the 'down' trough rises to stop the water running out of the end but offers little obstruction to a scoop being lifted late. No doubt the crew will take the opportunity to fill the tender. Trains on this service avoided Temple Meads, stopping at Stapleton Road instead.

33. Carrying an express passenger headcode, 'Bulldog' class 4—4—0 No. 3396 *Natal Colony* hurries a 'B'-set over Fox's Wood water troughs. The 'B'-set is made-up of a pair of identical non-corridor brake composite coaches to diagram E140, of which Bristol Division received a large proportion. It will be seen the leading coach carries the wording of 'BRISTOL DIVISION TRAIN No. —', of which the last part cannot be seen.

34. Having now got the road, No. 5118, a '5101' class large prairie 2—6—2T, heads its train out of the 'down' goods loop at Patchway station. No. 5118 started life as No. 3118 until it was renumbered in May 1928. It has received a new lower cab but has not been fitted with outside steampipes. It was withdrawn in March 1938 and its frames used to produce No. 8102, which was completed in June of the same year. The wagons are of interest, the first four belonging to 'Baldwin', followed by a GW 'Open C' and a very clean GLM wagon.

35. The eastern portal of the Severn Tunnel is the setting, as an 'up' freight emerges headed by a pair of tank engines. The leading engine is begrimed from constant use through the tunnel to assist 'up' and 'down' freights. The pilot is '3150' class No. 3174 and the train engine is '42XX' class 2—8—0T No. 5243. The boiler of No. 3174 has been fitted at some time to a locomotive with outside steam pipes. Some very distinctive vehicles can be seen in the train. On a number of coke wagons, extension rails are fitted which are as high as the van following. The board above the Severn Tunnel East signal box is a sighting board for a signal higher up to the right out of view, whilst the signal on the left has its own smaller version. These were required because it was difficult to see signals against the embankment and tunnel portal.

36. A pair of engines blast out of Ableton Lane Tunnel with an 'up' freight. This tunnel is a short one of only 97 yards and is immediately to the east of the Severn Tunnel. Headed by a '3150' class 2—6—2T as pilot, the train engine is a '28XX' class 2—8—0. The pilot will come off at Pilning, its duty duly completed, although it may then have to bank the train to Patchway. Note the pilot engine number on the disc above the buffer beam of the '3150'.

37. 'Star' class 4–6–0 No. 4043 *Prince Henry* begins the descent from Patchway station towards the Severn Tunnel with a west to north express. The engine, built in May 1913, is in excellent condition. It was fitted with new outside cylinders and 'Castle'-style steampipes in October 1931. The train is interesting in that the first two vehicles are slightly out of the ordinary, the first is a clerestory saloon of diagram G18, possibly privately hired; saloons like this were kept at major centres for such use. Next is a diagram K38 passenger brake van lettered 'Ocean Mails' built in 1926 on Lot 1346. At this point the 'up' line is just to the left of the train in the cutting, the track visible is the 'up' goods refuge siding.

38. We see an unusual double-heading of an 'up' express near Claverham. The reason for this is not obvious, although the 'Castle' class may be having a problem and the 2–6–0 is assisting. This latter locomotive, No. 4349, is a Taunton engine so is working away from its home shed; its tender is fitted with a tablet exchange fitting for use on the Barnstaple line.

39. A low angle photograph of the renamed *King George VI* No. 6028 at the head of the 3.30 p.m. Paddington to Penzance express leaving Westbury station. Formerly *King Henry II*, it was renamed in January 1937. If the train is in fact moving, the lack of smoke or steam is impressive. A couple of interesting wagons can be seen on the right; one with grease axle boxes belonging to John Shaw and Co. of Glastonbury.

40. No. 6027 *King Richard I* heads west into the sun with a 'down' express through Westbury. The coach in the view is No. 3795, which was built on Lot 1278 to diagram D69 in October 1920 and was a steel panelled 70' 'toplight' brake third. On the right is an interesting array of signals protecting the approaches to Westbury. Alongside of this, in the 'up' main line, can be seen an ATC ramp.

43. It is 3.15 p.m. on a sunny day at Bristol Temple Meads. On the concourse passengers await trains under the magnificent curved roof, completed in 1876. This part of the station was built to replace the two terminal stations which existed at right angles to each other, one being Brunel's original GW building, the other belonging to the Bristol & Exeter Railway. The photograph is taken from Platform 10, which was the west end of Platform 9. The scissor crossover which allowed this double use can be clearly seen in the foreground. Opposite is Platform 7.

Opposite page top:
41. A panoramic view of the recently rebuilt Temple Meads station taken from the southern end. It is possible to place a lot of the photographs taken by Mr. Soole around Temple Meads in this view. On the left may be seen the end-loading docks, in front of the former Bristol & Exeter Railway station building. The first passenger platform is No. 11, with its run-round facility, used for the Portishead trains. Next is Platform 10, with a goods train passing through on the 'up' loop. Platforms 8 and 6 are the shorter ones in the middle, those pointing towards the camera are Nos. 5 and 4, the best for train spotting! To the right, with a local '4575' class 2—6—2T hauled train, are platforms 2 and 1. The tracks leading into Bath Road engine shed curve away to the right and are in front of the brick-built signal box.

Opposite page bottom:
42. A high angle photograph of the north end of Bristol Temple Meads station. Identification of the view from left to right is as follows: The end of platforms 6 and 7 with spur No. 1 which has a 6-plank wagon standing on it. Between Platform 7 and Platform 9/10 are the through roads which allowed trains to pass through and engines to be changed without using the platform lines. An 'up' express is standing in Platform 9/10 awaiting its locomotive, which is a 'Castle' class 4—6—0 coming through on the 'up' loop line. To the right of the water tank are the suburban platforms 12/13 on the left and 14/15 on the right with a train standing awaiting departure. Further to the right is Temple Meads goods yard and sheds. The line passing the outer wall of Brunel's station goes through to the docks and Redcliffe goods yard.

44. This interesting view was taken from Bristol East signal box looking at Midland Junction and towards Dr. Day's carriage sidings and Junction. The tracks to the left are the LMS lines coming in from Gloucester, while those going straight on are, from left to right: 'Up' and 'down' relief lines for Filton, 'up' relief, 'up' main, 'down' main and 'down' relief. It will be seen that the 'up' and 'down' main lines split at Dr. Day's Junction, one set turning towards the left and Filton, the other set running with the relief lines on either side to Bath. These form two sides of a triangle. The third side can just be seen below the large chimneys. To the right, through the colour light signal gantry, can be seen Kingsland Road goods depot, with a pannier tank working the sidings. In the carriage sidings can be seen rakes of coaches, a fair percentage of which are clerestory vehicles awaiting their next duty. Note the old single-arc 6-wheeled carriage body now grounded and used as a mess room.

45. This photograph is a view from the Bristol West signal box looking towards Bedminster. Pyle Hill goods depot is on the right. The yard is full of open wagons and vans of which a large percentage are GW. This depot was only about half a mile from the main goods station on the north side of Temple Meads station. In the carriage sidings stands a Post Office van of diagram L22, next to it a high sided 6-wheeled Siphon of diagram O5. On the left can be seen the rear of a freight train negotiating the point-work on the avoiding line via St. Philips Marsh. The tracks at this point are, left to right, 'up' and 'down' avoiding, 'down' relief, 'down' main, 'up' main and 'up' relief. The remainder are goods reception or running lines.

46. A view of what was Britain's largest goods shed. It was sited alongside the north-eastern end of Bristol Temple Meads station. The signal box visible to the left of centre controls the line down to Redlands goods depot and the Floating Harbour. Just at the left of the picture can be seen part of the 1876 extension of the old Brunel station. After the rebuilding of the 1930s this was used as a station for local services. On shed can be seen an interesting selection of goods vehicles, some of which are being shunted on the right. Among the wagons visible are a 'Mink F' and a 'Mica'. Standing overall may be seen the imposing spire of the church of St. Mary Redcliffe.

47. A view of the south-western end of Bristol Temple Meads is seen from underneath Bath Road bridge. On the right can be seen Bristol West signal box and through the right-hand part of the bridge is Bath Road engine shed. On shed can be seen tool van No. 38, a locomotive coal wagon, a 'Bulldog' class 4—4—0 and a '57XX' pannier tank with a brake van, which is passing the Locomotive Yard signal box. Through the second-from-left section of the bridge is a 'Castle' class locomotive. To the left may be seen some spare coaches and a 6-wheeled Siphon.

48. The time is 1.30 p.m., the place Temple Meads forecourt. Buses and cars stand waiting, while in the passage below three LMS/GW joint lorries stand outside the premises of W. E. Coombs and a couple of men lean against some barrels having a chat. The lorries on the left are two Thornycrofts and an early Scammel 'mechanical horse'. Among the cars in the forecourt are Vauxhalls and a Lancia. The larger bus is a 'Bristol', whilst the hotel transport belonging to the 'Grand Hotel and Grand Spa Hotel, Clifton' is either an early Bedford or a Chevrolet. This photograph was taken from the old Control Office.

49. An 'up' express is waiting at Platform 9 at Bristol Temple Meads as 4–6–0 No. 4037 *The South Wales Borderers* reverses on to the train in readiness for departure time. No. 4037 was originally a 'Star' class engine built in 1910 and named *Queen Philippa*. She was withdrawn in June 1926 and rebuilt as a 'Castle' class engine, retaining her original name until March 1937 when she was renamed as photographed. The locomotive is equipped with a speedometer, although not all of the class were at this time. In the suburban platforms can be seen a '4575' class small prairie with a 'B'-set branded 'Bristol Division Train No. 9', which identifies it as being comprised of coaches Nos. 6551 and 6553, each of diagram E129. Note the accessories: fire-devil stove, bicycle, platform trolleys, etc.

50. A very smoky Bath Road shed provides the background for this study of No. 5032 *Usk Castle*. She is standing on the 'down' middle road adjacent to Platform 4. The unique tender, No. 2586, is shown here in rear view. The body was a standard 4000 gallon unit but the chassis carried eight 3' wheels instead of the normal six 3' 6" or 4' 0" diameter types. It carries the 'shirt-button' monogram.

51. St. Philips Marsh shed at Bristol is the setting for this photograph of No. 111 *Viscount Churchill*. The locomotive was the rebuild of the GW pacific *The Great Bear*. As is probably well-known this took place when the inner firebox was due for renewal on *The Great Bear*. C. B. Collett decided that because of that and the locomotive's limited route availability, a rebuild to a 'Castle' class was the best solution. In fact very little of the original engine was used when the work commenced in January 1924. A point to note is that at this date the locomotive did not carry the additional 'Castle' class plate below the nameplate. The smokebox cleaning taking place here was one of the less pleasant duties of the shed staff.

Opposite page top:
52. The village of Somerton is just visible at the extreme left behind the last coach in this photograph of the 'up' Cornish Riviera Limited. At the head of the train is 'King' class No. 6027 *King Richard I* which looks as if it did not receive the normal cleaning before the journey. With the exception of the first and last 'strengthening' coaches, the rake is of clean modern vehicles mainly of the 'centenary' type. This photograph captures what most people think of as *the* Great Western. If this was in colour how well the train would compliment the summer countryside.

Opposite page bottom:
53. A rather grubby 'Castle' class locomotive pulls away from Horfield station with an 'up' local stopping train. Whilst the engine is carrying a 'B' code, the carriages have nameboards and are certainly not the usual types found on local trains, they are all corridor types. No. 4095 *Harlech Castle* was built in June 1926 and still has the older tender insignia of 'Great (crest) Western'. The brick bridge carries Bonnington Walk. The tracks on the left are the fast or main lines and the slow or relief lines on the right.

54. A 'down' express near Long Ashton passes under Ashton Brook aquaduct as it heads west. The locomotive is 'Castle' class No. 4092 *Dunraven Castle* and has nine coaches in its train. Note the leading coach, which is a brake third to diagram D118, has only one door with a droplight in each double door set. Otherwise it was identical to diagram D116.

55. The quarry at Fox's Wood is the setting for this photograph of an 'up' Brighton-Cardiff train hauled by 'Star' class 4—6—0 No. 4033 *Queen Victoria*. The engine has just finished taking water from the trough, the end of which is just beneath the tender. A Siphon 'G' van of diagram O11 is still dripping water from its leading 9′ American bogie after its drenching from the spray of the water pick-up. The sign on the far side of the track in front of the engine is the commencement notice for the 'up' trough. In the foreground, the tracks belong to the quarry, the transfer line being just to this side of the main line. Among the debris is a narrow gauge side-tipper wagon.

56. Patchway station viewed from the 'down' goods loop headshunt. Passing through the station at the head of a 'down' express is No. 4091 *Dudley Castle*. In the 'down' goods loop, a '28XX' class 2−8−0 heavy freight locomotive waits for a clear road for its train. The engine's crew watch Mr. Soole while leaning against the signal, presumably after contacting the signal box on the telephone mounted on the signal post. Note that the headshunt is separately signalled.

57. The domed nose of No. 5005 *Manorbier Castle* reflects the sun as the locomotive reaches the summit at Patchway station after several miles of climbing. The partially streamlined 'Castle' class locomotive is heading an 'up' express. A freight train stands in the 'up' refuge siding awaiting its turn to continue its journey. We can see that No. 5005 has lost some of its panels, notably those around the front end, which caused problems during maintenance and of overheating. The track with the new ballast in the foreground is the headshunt for the 'down' goods loop.

58. This photograph shows just how steep the pull up to Patchway station from the tunnel is, the 'down' main line through the left arch of the bridge being less severe. With a little more work still to do 'Castle' class No. 5010 *Restormel Castle* enters the station with an 'up' express. The first coach is a clerestory saloon to diagram G33 and note that there are at least four other clerestory vehicles in this train. To the left a 'down' freight moves along the goods loop. It is signalled forward into the headshunt and this allows the brake van to clear the facing connection at the start of the loop. Note the two different patterns of ground disc signals between the tracks and also the ATC ramp in the 'down' track after the boardwalk.

59. Approaching Narroways Hill Junction is No. 4025 *Italian Monarch* of the 'Star' class. No. 4025 was originally called *King Charles* when built in July 1909, but it lost this name to the 'King' class in October 1927. Its new title was removed in June 1940 for obvious reasons and remained unnamed until withdrawal. The style which No. 4025 displays in this photograph, tall safety valve cover with top feed, tall chimney and small 3500 gallon tender represents these locomotives at their most elegant. Behind the locomotive are two identical brake composites of diagram E148 the first being No. 6918. Both sides of this type are visible here, note the corridor side does not provide one door per compartment. This was an interim cost reduction prior to abandonment of compartment doors on later stock. On the right can be seen new houses built on recently levelled ground in the area of Mullers Road.

60. A 'down' express passes near Somerton headed by 'King' class No. 6015 *King Richard III*. The train bears out the often made criticism of the GWR train make-up; it comprises coaches of different age and design. The earliest vehicle is the 'Concertina' diner which was built in 1907 and the newest is the leading brake third of 1934 type. It would appear the ballast may have been recently replaced as there is old ballast on the side of the embankment.

61. Here we see another interesting overall view of the east end of Stoke Gifford yard. The 'up' express passing through the yard is hauled by a 'Star' class 4–6–0 which, according to the NRM index, is No. 4028 *Roumanian Monarch*. This locomotive was originally named *King John* until the name was transferred to the 'King' class in 1927. This photograph, with all the private owner wagons in the sidings, would have been very interesting had it been in colour.

62. Taken in late 1936/early 1937, this photograph shows 'Star' class No. 4064 *Reading Abbey* fitted with a 4000 gallon tender passing Fllton goods yard on its way out of Bristol. *Reading Abbey* was rebuilt as a 'Castle' class in early 1937, being withdrawn in the February and reappearing in April. At the rear of the train are two vehicles of note. The second from last coach is one of the luxurious 'Super Saloons' of diagram G60. These vehicles were especially constructed for the 'Ocean' traffic, providing the Great Western with a carriage of Pullman quality, without the associated problems. Eight of these magnificent coaches were built after Pullmans had been tried on certain services for a couple of years. All eight vehicles were given names or titles of members of the Royal Family, which were emblazoned in large letters along the sides. The last coach appears to have been very recently outshopped. It's not a new carriage, the GWR built the last 70′ vehicles some ten years earlier and this one looks to be a Collett 70′ third.

63. Judging by the flowers growing on the embankments this photograph was taken in the spring or summer. It shows 4–6–0 No. 5029 *Nunney Castle* blasting its way up the hill from Patchway Tunnel under the A38 roadbridge in 1937. One wonders how many motorists have crossed this bridge not knowing what lies below. The leading vehicle, a 'toplight' steel-panelled third, has recently had a repaint. The white roofs were soon discoloured with soot and ash from locomotives.

64. The 5.15 p.m. express to Paddington passes Narroways Hill Junction on the climb out of Bristol towards Filton Junction, where it turns east towards the capital. No. 5031 *Totnes Castle* heads the train composed of standard carriage stock, as it passes under the footbridge and is about to pass under the LMS line (for Clifton Down). Built in 1934, No. 5031 was fitted with a fire iron tunnel from new. In the foreground the relief line has a seep or drain under it, a common occurrence.

65. An 'up' express runs along the 'up' relief line past Narroways Hill Junction. The locomotive, 'Star' class No. 4068 *Llanthony Abbey*, was built in January 1923 and is now equipped with a 4000 gallon tender. This locomotive was withdrawn and rebuilt in February 1939 as a 'Castle' class No. 5088. Behind the 6-wheeled milk van, of LSWR origin, are two full brakes of diagram K38, the first labelled 'Ocean Mails' on the lower body panels.

66. The south end of Patchway station is seen with a 'down' express passing bound for Bristol. The locomotive is No. 5034 *Corfe Castle* built in May 1935 and shedded at Newton Abbot about this time, so it will probably be working home with this north to west express. This photograph was taken from the platform and steps which were built to allow the guard of a freight train put into the 'down' loop, to signal his engine crew. The 'down' loop here had a headshunt and a tailshunt. When a train too long for the basic loop was signalled in, the locomotive would go forward into the headshunt and the guard would signal to the crew when his van was clear of the points for the tailshunt. The train would then reverse back into the tailshunt, so that when given the right-away, it could pull out of the loop onto the 'down' main line. Behind No. 5034 can be seen Patchway signal box which controlled Patchway loops and the junction to Bristol and London. Next to the box is the small goods shed and office. Of the two coal wagons visible, the left-hand one is interesting in that its home base was Patchway; it belonged to Hayward and Barton, coal merchants.

67. A view along Patchway station with 'Castle' class No. 5010 *Restormel Castle* passing through on an 'up' ex-South Wales express heading for London. The junction signal can just be seen under the footbridge, as can also a 'down' freight awaiting a clear road. This train is standing in the 'down' goods loop behind the platform on the left.

69. An 'up' ex-South Wales parcels train runs past Patchway Tunnel signal box after passing under the A38 road bridge. The train engine with a good pall of smoke is No. 3392 *New Zealand* of the 'Bulldog' class, whilst the pilot, No. 1 for that day, is '3150' class 2–6–2T No. 3176. Both locomotives appear to have shut off steam, although there is still about a quarter of a mile to the summit on a gradient of about 1 in 80. The pilot engine will be detached from the train at Patchway station and will return for another job. On the right above No. 3176 can be seen the gate and pathway for the signalmen to gain access to their box.

Opposite page:
68. A rather dirty No. 5013 *Abergavenny Castle* stands with its train in Bristol Temple Meads Platform 9. This locomotive was the first 'Castle' built with the box-type inner cylinder covers when it was completed in 1932. It was also the first 'Castle' built for nearly five years, on Lot 280, a batch which introduced several new features to the class. The engine is in back gear and therefore has just backed onto the train and is probably being coupled up, 'leaning' on the first coach to assist the operation. Behind the tender is coach No. 5196 built to diagram C58 on Lot 1411 in May 1929. The roof of the Victorian extension to Brunel's terminus station, with its ornate wrought iron work and castellated turrets, contrast with its angular 20th century neighbour — the water tank. To the right of the tank can be seen part of the huge goods depot.

70. This interesting photograph, taken at Newton Abbot station, shows small prairie No. 5557 standing at Platform 5. The engine has reversed onto the train and the fireman has just climbed back onto the platform having removed the tail lamp. The leading coach of the train has recently been out-shopped as its roof is still quite white. On the left can be seen a 'toplight' 70' first class coach of diagram A13.

72. The shape of things to come. The Great Western were one of the first companies to realise the potential of diesels for railways. Several previous attempts at introducing self-propelled coaches had been made, the most successful of these was the steam rail motor, the last of which were being withdrawn as the first diesel railcars entered service. In collaboration with A.E.C. and Park Royal, the GW's first railcar was completed in 1933. No. 1 can be looked upon as the beginning of the end of steam traction. Indeed the sleek lines wouldn't look out of place today. Given the diagram U, this vehicle was always different to later batches, the most obvious changes being with the doors to the driving compartment. On later units, the driver used the passenger entrance, but as can be seen here, the driver's access on No. 1 was through side doors. Seen here on the slow line near Maidenhead, these vehicles were often used over quite long distances, as mini-expresses, such as the Cardiff-Birmingham and Bristol-Weymouth trains.

Opposite page bottom:
71. Approaching Stoke Gifford round the curve from Filton Junction is a '517' class 0–4–2T with two non-corridor clerestory coaches. The time of day and stock suggest that this is a workmen's train, taking a new shift of workers to Stoke Gifford goods yard. The locomotive, No. 1163, was built at Wolverhampton Works in March 1876. Like most of its class it had a rather complicated life. The wheelbase was increased and outside bearing-type rear wheels fitted at Swindon in August 1895. Other modifications were to the boiler type, addition of an enclosed cab, enlarged bunker and side tanks. It was also one of the class which was painted in carriage livery under G. J. Churchward to match the autocoaches for which autogear was also fitted. The carriages are an E45 diagram ex-brake tri-composite, which had a semi-corridor and was sometimes used as a slip-coach, the other is one of the many diagram C10 third class vehicles.

75. An 'up' freight passes under the A38 road bridge, its banker just emerging from the Patchway long tunnel. At its head, looking smart in its plain green and black livery, 2−6−0 No. 4377 pulls briskly up to Patchway where the banking engine will detach. The train is a typical mixed freight, in this case carrying goods from South Wales. The difference between the levels of the 'up' and 'down' lines is very apparent in this view, the 'up' line having an easier gradient to assist ascending trains. 'Down' trains continue into the cutting seen through the second from left arch, before entering a shorter tunnel than the 'up' line. The notice board demands all 'down' goods trains to stop and the guards to pin-down the wagons' brakes for the descent.

Opposite page top:
73. Pictured when only a few months old, No. 6820 *Kingstone Grange* works a 'down' empty coal train towards the Severn Tunnel. It is pictured just after Patchway station. No. 6820 was built in January 1937 and was shedded at Newport Ebbw Junction and is therefore working home. The 'Grange' class were very popular locomotives with the traffic department and crews. Although constructed in 1936, usually with some parts recovered from scrapped '43XX' class 2−6−0s, the design was originally envisaged in 1901 in Churchward's Master Plan. With their large boilers and small wheels they were used with excellent results on hilly and twisting routes as in Devon and Cornwall, being equally at home with passenger or freight trains as we can see here. An interesting selection of wagons can be seen including a 'Bedwas' coke wagon and six GW locomotive coal wagons.

Opposite page bottom:
74. One of the early 'Saint' class locomotives No. 2902 *Lady of the Lake*, in almost original condition, heads a 'down' empty milk train towards South Wales. It was photographed on the curve between Stoke Gifford and Patchway and has almost reached the junction with the line from Bristol. No. 2902 was in fact the last of the survivors of the square 'drop-end' Saints to receive new outside steampipe cylinders and hence curved drop-ends. She was condemned 43 years after completion and outlived many of her sisters. The 6-wheeled van is an ex-Taff Vale Railway PBV inherited by the GW after the grouping of 1923.

76. Streamlined 'King' class No. 6014 *King Henry VII* is photographed near Horfield on the four-track section between Filton Junction and Bristol. The uniform rake of stock on the 'up' Bristolian this day looks especially neat. It contrasts with the reputation the GW had of always having vehicles of different age and styles in its trains. The centre carriage is a buffet car, of diagram H41.

77. The 'up' Torbay Limited hurries along the troughs at Fairwood near Westbury. In charge of the train on this day is No. 6009 *King Charles II* which is replenishing its tank. It is possible to see the way the tracks dip into the troughs behind the train where they begin. The troughs were replenished from two water tanks, one for the 'up' and one for the 'down' line. Mr. Soole was using the top of the 'down' tank to take this view. The neat 'pavé' was used to protect the under ballast from erosion due to the spray from the water pick-up.

78. 'Star' class 4—6—0 No. 4022 *Belgian Monarch* was named *King William* until June 1927. It heads an express out of Bristol Temple Meads, passing Dr. Day's Junction before climbing to Filton Junction. There it will take either the route through the Severn Tunnel to South Wales and the north, or turn east towards London. Of note behind the train are the long colour-light signal gantries which were installed when the station was rebuilt and a goods train in the distance.

79. 'Castle' class 4—6—0 No. 5039 *Rhuddlan Castle* brings a Weston-Super-Mare to Paddington train into Bristol Temple Meads under Bath Road Bridge. The train is approaching Platform 10 with a brown passenger brake van (diagram K40) at its head. Towering over the whole scene are the houses of Totterdown which must have given any train spotters living there a fine view. Beyond No. 5039, standing in the confines of the locomotive depot, is a Mess & Tool van, No. 31.

80. An 'up' express speeds across the Somerset flats near Claverham. In charge of the train is 'Star' class 4—6—0 No. 4020 *Knight Commander*, which is still equipped with a 3500 gallon tender. It must be a warm summer evening as most of the coaches have the droplights down and a number of passengers are taking the air or admiring the view.

81. The late evening sun highlights a west to north express near Claverham as it heads towards Bristol. The coaches are an odd mixture of LMS (which includes some ex-LNWR stock), GW and some miscellaneous vans at the rear. The locomotive was the first of four of the 'Castle' class to carry the name *Ogmore Castle* and is No. 5056. It was completed in June 1936 and only carried this name for fifteen months when it was renamed *Earl of Powis*.

82. With steam to spare 'Hall' class 4—6—0 No. 4999 *Gopsal Hall*, which was built in March 1931, nears the summit at Patchway with a north to west express. No. 4999 is working home to Plymouth and has more testing banks ahead in Devon. The boiler lagging band behind the smokebox has the joint at the top which was done to make fitting easier. Previously these joints had all been below the boiler. Note that the new ballast recently dropped on the 'up' line appears almost white.

83. Smoke still obscures the east portal of Patchway long tunnel as a Cardiff-Brighton train continues its climb to the summit at Patchway station. It is seen here passing under the A38 road bridge. The train is of Southern Railway stock, with a GWR outside-framed Siphon 'G' at the rear. The locomotive is 4—6—0 No. 4044 *Prince George* of the 'Star' class. No. 4044 is equipped with an intermediate 3500 gallon tender. A 'down' freight descends on the left towards the shorter tunnel.

86. Westbury again with 'Castle' class No. 5013 *Abergavenny Castle* seen at the head of the 3.30 p.m. Paddington-Penzance express comprised mostly of 70′ stock. The lovely bracket signal, operated from Westbury south box, controls the approaches from the west. The lower left arm indicates the route into the sidings, its companion covers the 'up' goods running loop. On the tall centre post are the 'up' main line home and distant through the station. Adjacent to this, the right-hand arm controls the crossover to the 'up' Salisbury platform.

Opposite page top:
84. 'King' class No. 6027 *King Richard I* comes off the Westbury avoiding line and passes Fairwood Junction signal box. The train is the 'down' Torbay Limited and is just passing a speed restriction termination sign on the right. It would appear that the signal box is rather dirty and may be due for a repaint. Note the signalman's bicycle.

Opposite page bottom:
85. The streamlined 'King', No. 6014 *King Henry VII*, leaves Westbury with a 'down' express. By this time the locomotive had lost the front-end fairings and also those on the tender. It carried the reporting number in the lower position to the end and also retained the wedge-fronted cab. On the right can be seen 'Toad' brake van No. 17778 of diagram AA2 built in 1910 on Lot 642. By this date it had been repainted with the 1937 small size of GW letters above the number, (this was standard between all four major railway companies).

87. A 'Castle' class heads west away from Bristol with the 11.15 a.m. Paddington-Weston-Super-Mare express, passing Pyle Hill goods depot. The locomotive is No. 5044 *Beverston Castle*, completed in March 1936, but renamed *Earl of Dunraven* in September 1937. Its original name was re-used in 1938 on No. 5068, completed in June of that year. The wagon experts will delight in the array of vehicles in the depot, several of LNER origin being visible. In the sidings above the first coach of the express are some 'spare' coaches and a Siphon. Colour light signals dominate the view and a colour light ground signal is seen below the locomotive's buffer. The train is running on the 'down' main line with the pair of tracks on the right being the 'up' and 'down' avoiding lines. Behind the train can be seen Bristol West signal box, Bath Road bridge and the roof of Bath Road engine shed is above the hoarding.

88. 'Castle' class No. 5036 *Lyonshall Castle* stands at Platform 4 at Bristol Temple Meads. It would appear that the fireman has not yet changed the headlamps from his journey from the carriage sidings. The low angle from which this photograph was taken shows the trackwork to and from platforms 1 and 2 on the right most effectively.

89. This photograph is an interesting view, it shows 'Star' class 4—6—0 No. 4038 *Queen Berengaria* approaching the Stoke Gifford end of the curve from Filton Junction with an 'up' local. At the extreme right is the main South Wales route from London curving round to Patchway. The Filton-Patchway line crosses the bridge seen in the distance behind the train. Under this bridge the two tracks, which are just to the right of the locomotive, head away to Severn Beach and Avonmouth. An old, possibly ex-TVR, tender is standing on some sidings which served a sludge tip. The carriages on the 'up' local are, we think, all Great Central Railway stock of elderly vintage. Certainly the third vehicle, a PBV and the fourth, a 1912 brake composite, are reasonably identifiable. Note that the locomotive has 'elbow' steampipes which were an early step-away from inside steampipes. The tender is an 'intermediate', one of ten built to lot A112 and numbered 2374-83. They were similar to the standard 3500 gallon type but with higher sides.

90. The roofs of the two clerestory coaches still show how the part below the rainstrip was brown, while that above was white. 4—6—0 No. 5011 *Tintagel Castle*, which was completed in July 1927, was shedded at Newton Abbot for most of its life and is therefore working home with this 'down'. train near Long Ashton.

92. We see a Royal Train composed of ex-LNWR Royal Saloons, still in LNWR colours. These coaches were used by the LMSR until 1941 and some for many years after. Unfortunately the Great Western Railway's 1897 Royal Train was down-graded from this premier role in the 1920s. The locomotive is No. 4082 *Windsor Castle* the 'Royal' engine. On either side of the smokebox are the two Royal crests which are now preserved, one being at Swindon Works. They are said to be one-piece castings, an interesting exercise in pattern-making! On the buffer beam are the special headlamps used on Royal trains. The event for which this train was running is not recorded, neither is the location, although it is possibly on the Westbury 'cut-off'. The formation of the train is a corridor brake first, a semi-Royal saloon, the two Royal King's and Queen's saloons, which were equipped with 6-wheeled bogies, two further semi-Royal saloons and what is probably the other corridor brake first.

Opposite page:

91. A 'down' north to west express passes through Stapleton Road station. It was quite common for these workings to have a number of horse-boxes in each direction. At the end of the extended platform (completed in 1917) is a water crane with its 'fire-devil' stove, used in the winter to prevent water freezing in the column. It will be noted that there is a metal plate under the burner to prevent the wooden platform being damaged. On the left is a corrugated iron lamp hut, used for storing supplies of oil, etc. for the station and signal lamps. The locomotive is 4—6—0 No. 5062 *Earl of Shaftsbury*. When completed in June 1937 it was named *Tenby Castle*, but was renamed as seen here, a few months later, in November of that year.

93. 'King' class 4—6—0 No. 6027 *King Richard I* simmers in the sunshine at Platforms 3/4 of Bristol Temple Meads station after bringing in the 'down' Bristolian. The platform clock shows the time. Above the leading brake third coach can be seen a pipe on the platform valance which was used to provide water to the roof tanks on the coaches. In fact valves can be seen at regular intervals along the valance for the same purpose.

94. Standing on the 'up' middle road between platforms 7 and 9 at Bristol Temple Meads is 'Hall' class No. 4945 *Milligan Hall*. The locomotive, with a horse-box of diagram N12 or N13 attached, is waiting to take over an 'up' express. On the tender the fireman takes the opportunity to sort out the coal prior to the journey, he also has the blower on, to prevent the engine blowing off. *Milligan Hall* was completed in August 1929 and has not yet received a 4000 gallon tender.

95. A photograph which shows off the lines of the 'King' class to perfection, No. 6003 *King George IV* rounds the curve from Filton Junction station at the head of the 'up' Bristolian. As the 'Castle' class were soon to take over this train, this and the other photographs of the Bristolian in this collection must have been taken shortly after the train's inception in the summer of 1935.

96. 'Saint' class 4—6—0 No. 2987 *Bride of Lammermoor* leaves Filton Junction station and heads towards Bristol with a stopping train from South Wales. This locomotive had a very interesting history. It was completed in August 1905 as a 4—4—2 and numbered 187, to make a comparison with the French engines and it received the name *Robertson* in the November of the same year. In April 1907 it was renamed as seen here, then in June 1912 was rebuilt as a 4—6—0 with curved drop ends to the frames in place of the original square pattern. It retained a lever reverser however. It will be seen that the locomotive has a boiler with provision for outside steampipes, a feature which No. 2987 did not receive until early 1942. The boiler had come off an engine already so fitted. The leading coach is worthy of note; a Dean clerestory, built at the end of the 1890s. It had a projection (a guard's look-out) in the brake end but these were removed during the late 1920s, (though by no means were they all altered) and the area covered with a steel sheet. This altered their diagram, in this case, from D30 to D72 or 73. The coach has also had its gas lighting replaced by electric lighting, again in the 1920s.

98. The driver of 'Castle' class 4—6—0 No. 5002 *Ludlow Castle* waves to Mr. Soole as his train enters Patchway station from South Wales. No. 5002 is rather grubby and is leaking steam from the inside cylinders. Note how short the post is on the signal at the end of the 'down' platform, this was so it could be seen under the footbridge. Also seen here is the use of old sections of bridge rail as track drain covers.

Opposite page:

97. A very interesting photograph indeed. The use of a '52XX' class on a passenger train is a most unusual occurrence, but the coaches themselves are also worthy of note. No. 5224 was one of Churchward's freight tank locomotives, built for the heavy coal trains of South Wales, being used for short journeys from pit to port. First built in 1910, the last of the class weren't completed until 1940, although by then a number had been enlarged and re-numbered into the '72XX' class. This particular example was built at Swindon in 1924. The leading coach was constructed under either Lot 983 or 988, which were later allocated diagram E72. These were 'through' coaches in the true sense, being semi-corridor with four WCs and used for services off the Great Western's system, to Liverpool, Dover, etc. Some were fitted with Westinghouse brake equipment for working over the northern routes. However, the vehicle seen here has been altered further, having had its guard's projection removed and electrical equipment fitted in place of the gas apparatus. The removal of the projection altered this coach into the diagram E119, one of only three to be recorded as such. The second carriage is to the diagram E25, another former tri-composite like the first coach, but this is an earlier vehicle, built in 1889-90 on Lot 483. Unusually, the arrangement of the compartments included two 'half' compartments at each end with small end windows, one for the first class at the luggage (far) end and the former second class one, at the nearer end. The second class was altered to third class in 1909 on these vehicles. All the E25s were condemned by mid-1936 and even when this photograph was taken in 1934, there weren't many left in service. Note that both coaches are fitted with different types of Dean bogies, the E72 having 10' versions, whilst the E25 has the smaller 6' 4" style. The recent work in quadrupling this section can be clearly seen, with older abutments on the left and the new ones to the right. Note also the ATC ramp in the foreground and the catch point.

99. With a train of mostly LMS stock 4–6–0 No. 5053 *Bishops Castle* takes the line for Patchway from Filton Junction station. The lines heading towards the bottom of the photograph curve round to the right towards Hallen Marsh Junction and Avonmouth.

100. The 5.15 p.m. Bristol-Paddington express passes Filton Junction goods depot. At its head is No. 5040 *Stokesay Castle*, which was used on several high speed runs by the GWR. The coaches are a uniform set of 1936/7 stock with a 1938 buffet car in the centre, its high window line contrasting with the others. Passing No. 5040 and its train, can be seen part of another 'down' passenger train. The vehicles in view are a 'toplight' 'Bars 1' composite of diagram E85, built in 1909 on Lot 1147 and a clerestory. To the right, above the wooden platform of the depot, may be seen an engine, but whether it is in the goods yard or on the 'up' relief cannot be determined. The bracket signal indicates that the express will turn east towards London, while the second lower arm on the same bracket, controls the main-to-relief crossing, which the train is approaching.

101. An 'up' freight passes Patchway Tunnel signal box on the ascent to the summit at Patchway station where the banking engine, out of sight but by its smoke has just left the tunnel, will drop off. The separation between the 'up' and 'down' lines is very apparent in this view. The train engine is a 42XX 2−8−0T No. 5245, which is signalled for a clear run through the station. However, the distant signal for Patchway Junction is 'on', which probably means the junction is being used. Tucked into the bank, between the tracks, is a platelayers hut.

102. '28XX' class No. 2810 in original condition blasts its way up the climb from Patchway Tunnel to the station with a 'D' class freight. It is banked in the rear by a '3150' class, the smoke from which can be seen in the top left. The train is made-up of wagons loaded with coal from South Wales. It will be noted that there are five GW locomotive coal wagons in the train, opposite the buffer stops of the 'up' refuge siding on the right. Also in the top left can be seen the rear of a 'down' goods heading for the tunnel.

103. This photograph poses a date problem! The location isn't in doubt, being Snyed Park Junction near Sea Mills on the Avonmouth line. Behind the train is the Avon Gorge. This line comes under the Downs from Clifton through a tunnel, the end of which is just out of sight around the bend. In the foreground on the right is the trackbed of the former Bristol Port and Pier Railway, which merged into a single track at this point and continued into the cutting behind the first telegraph pole. On the extreme right can be seen the river. The problem is that the railway from here to the terminus at Hotwells in the gorge, below the famous suspension bridge, was closed in July 1922. This was to make way for the construction of the A4 road, known as the Portway, which was completed in 1929. However, in this scene there is no sign of the road as there should be, as we estimate this photograph was taken in the summer of 1934. The train engine is a 'Bulldog', No. 3376 *River Plym*, heading a 'down' local towards Avonmouth. The leading vehicle is one of interest. Constructed on Lot 697 in 1893-4, these coaches were known as 'Falmouth Coupés' and later given the diagram E39. Built as semi-corridor stock, they were popular as through coaches as each compartment had access to a toilet.

104. The coal on the tender is stacked as high as the cab of No. 4096 *Highclere Castle* as it starts the long descent to the Severn Tunnel with an express. The leading coach is a 40' passenger brake van which has had its guard's side look-outs or projections removed and a steel plate fitted in their place. This plate reads 'PASSENGER PARCELS VAN'. As will be seen from the roof, this vehicle is still equipped with gas lighting and is in brown livery.

105. No. 5040 *Stokesay Castle* approaches Pilning with an 'up' express of very mixed stock. The rear vehicle is a 70′ mail van so the train is probably a Fishguard to London one. The 'concertina' coaches would also bear this out since they were used on this route for most of their existence. *Stokesay Castle* was a fairly new locomotive when this photograph was taken, being completed in June 1935. It was shedded at Old Oak Common for most of its life. To the right, in the siding on the embankment, is a 45′ open carriage truck, telegraphic code name Scorpion 'C' of diagram P11, of which eight were built. These vehicles were to transport road vehicles through the Severn Tunnel, between Severn Tunnel Junction and Pilning, attached to the rear of passenger trains.

106. The premier locomotive of the Great Western Railway is made ready at Old Oak Common for a special occasion. The time is in the early hours of the 29th November 1934 and No. 6000 *King George V* is to haul a special train for Princess Marina's wedding. The group of officials on the right are no doubt discussing the arrangements. Note how the souvenir bell from the Baltimore & Ohio Railroad Co. shines in the early morning light. Of interest also is the 40 ton locomotive coal wagon No. 53965 awaiting its turn in the coaling stage.

107. An unusual view of the southern end of Bristol Temple Meads taken from the old Bristol and Exeter Railway offices. On the left in Platform 11 is a Portishead local train headed by a '4575' class small prairie. Its train is made-up of a 'B'-set of diagram E129 and an early clerestory third of diagram C3. Note the Dean 6' 4" bogies which retain the lower footboards. In the bay platforms in the centre are a 5-plank wagon, a GW horse box, two LMS PBVs, a van and a number of Siphons of various types. Beyond on Bath Road engine shed can be seen three 'Castles', a 'Dean Goods', part of a 'Hall' and a '4575'. To the right is Bath Road bridge under which passes the main line to the west.

108. Fairwood troughs are seen with the 'up' Torbay Express, hauled by 'King' class locomotive No. 6024 *King Edward I*. The fireman is replenishing the tender water tank from the trough as can be seen by the spray. Note the water lying in the edge of the ballast on the 'down' line and also the neat haystack in the field on the right. By the amount of spray in the air, Mr. Soole would not have escaped without a wetting.

109. An unusual but interesting rear view of No. 6009 *King Charles II* just passing Fairwood Junction. The train is taking the Westbury avoiding line, the other tracks behind the engine lead into Westbury. The locomotive has just picked up water from the troughs as the tender top is still wet and so is the leading coach. It is hoped that the corridor connection blanking board of No. 5199 was fitted, if not, the effect of taking-on water could be very frightening for the passengers! The coach was of diagram C58, built in 1929 on Lot 1411. The fireman appears to have the right-hand live steam injector running, taking advantage of the full tank and good steam pressure.

110. A north to west express crosses the bridge over Stapleton Road and is about to enter the station of the same name. This girder bridge was erected when the tracks here were quadrupled in 1891. The tracks, which can be seen on the left, cross an ordinary bridge, whereas the bridge seen here is of three spans and carries the main lines. The locomotive is 4—6—0 No. 5028 *Llantilo Castle*, which was completed in May 1934. It has since been fitted with a speedometer.

111. The signals have been reset quickly behind 4—6—0 No. 5027 *Farleigh Castle* as it approaches Bedminster with a 'down' express. It is at this point that the avoiding lines around to the south of Temple Meads station and those through the station, join. This allows freight and other trains to continue without entering the station confines and assisted the traffic department. Also feeding off the avoiding line was the large locomotive shed St. Philips Marsh. The rusty track in the foreground is a trap, protecting the main lines.

112. No. 5047 *Compton Castle* at the head of an 'up' express covers the last half mile of the climb towards Patchway station. Built in April 1936 No. 5047 was renamed *Earl of Dartmouth* in August 1937, so was nearly new when photographed by Mr. Soole. The first coach in the train is unusual, it is a brake third converted to a buffet car by altering two compartments to a kitchen and pantry. Two coaches were altered, one a diagram D46, No. 2365, becoming diagram H18, the other a diagram D47, No. 2355, becoming diagram H17. Both were returned to ordinary traffic in April 1934 and reconverted in 1936 to brake thirds. The second vehicle is also a diner and is one of the flat sided vehicles built to diagram H24 in 1922. On the left at a higher level a 'down' freight train is stopped at the board which demands all freight and mineral trains to stop dead to allow the brakes to be pinned down for the descent.

113. The driver of 'Castle' class No. 4075 *Cardiff Castle* watches from the cab of his engine on an 'up' express as Mr. Soole takes a picture of his train near Patchway station. Behind the locomotive is one of the brake thirds of diagram D121 which, along with third (diagram C70) and composite (diagram E151) were unusual in having vehicle numbers and class markings on the cream, rather than the brown, because of the very low waistline. Above the locomotive can be seen the end of the 'up' goods refuge siding.

115. A highly polished 'King' class 4—6—0 No. 6025 *King Henry III* leaves Bristol with a 'down' express. On the extreme left is Pyle Hill goods depot, while on the right on top of the embankment are the houses of Totterdown. Behind the engine are three coaches, which are presumably being worked back to the west country. The first is a 'Riviera' kitchen car (diagram H35), the second a 'Riviera' dining saloon, the third is 'Super Saloon' No. 9117 *Princess Royal* (diagram H45). Also in the train is the diagram H11 dining car with the large bogies, No. 9505. This is the sixth carriage, which is · behind the twin colour light signal. On the right can be seen the wagons on a train running on the avoiding lines.

Opposite page:
114. A recently overhauled 'Hall' class locomotive on a running-in turn from Swindon works. It is fully lined and is in pristine condition. The engine, No. 4926 *Farleigh Hall*, was built in May 1929. Its Swindon-Bristol local train is a 'B'-set, each coach of which is to diagram E140. It will be noted that the platforms have been extended with wooden surface and frame assemblies. One can also see that GWR locomotive lamps were to the side of the lamp brackets. The other three major companies' engine lamps were in front of their lamp-brackets.

116. Taken from the west end of Pyle Hill carriage sidings, the 12.00 a.m. Penzance to Crewe express is photographed standing awaiting clearance to enter Bristol Temple Meads. Both the crew members of No. 4094 *Dynevor Castle* are watching Mr. Soole. The boys who can be seen above the TPO have obviously seen it all before. It was from this same vantage point that Mr. Soole took some of his photographs. The train was one of those which wandered in seemingly lazy fashion. Leaving Penzance around midday, it picked up the mail van and the first coach, a 'concertina' 70' third, at Plymouth, detaching them at Bristol. The following three vehicles, a GW brake-composite, Siphon 'G', and LMS brake-third, went on to Crewe, leaving Bristol at 7.20 p.m. and arriving there at 11.20 p.m. The two GW vehicles were then forwarded to Liverpool, while the LMS carriage went on to Manchester. The train also carried a GW through coach to Glasgow.

117. The driver of the '57XX' class 0–6–0PT working at the Kingsland goods depot watches as an 'up' express, headed by 'Star' class 4–6–0 No. 4055 *Princess Sophia*, passes by heading for Filton Junction. On the right, behind signal No. 3, is Dr. Day's carriage sidings, on which can be seen a former full-brake being used as a stores van. This is one built to diagram K2. The semaphore signal seen just in front of No. 4055 protects the junction with the GWR of the former LMS line from Barrow Hill, which was built by the Bristol and Gloucester Railway.

118. Two engines approach Pilning station with an 'up' coal train from South Wales. The leading engine is a pilot from Severn Tunnel Junction, No. 3159 of the '3150' class, which was used virtually exclusively for banking duties. At Pilning the pilot engine dropped off into the refuge siding, the train moved forward and the pilot then became a banker up to the summit at Patchway. The train engine is an early member of the '28XX' class, in fact one of the 2800-30 batch which had a square drop end to the front of the footplate. A signal situated on the wrong side of the track is off and so a 'down' train is imminent. Signals were placed in this way to allow drivers a clear view past obstructions, in this case Pilning station, from the right-hand driving position of GW engines.

119. A 'down' train rumbles through the Somerset countryside behind a '28XX' class 2—8—0 heavy goods locomotive. The hill in the background is Brent Knoll, a well-known landmark standing out from the Somerset levels. No. 2819, built in December 1905, was one of the early members of the class, but had had its front end renewed in June 1935 when it received new cylinders with outside steampipes and also a cast iron chimney. The train has ten 6-wheeled Siphons at its head. This was unusual for the class of train. Possibly they were being worked back empty, for redistribution.

120. No. 4923 *Evenley Hall* heads a 'down' express through Patchway station towards South Wales. The locomotive was built in April 1929 and still has the original type of tender. The leading coach is of interest. It was built as a tri-composite and had three toilets and a guard's compartment. It was the last design of vehicle with guard's look-outs or projections and in fact the only elliptically-roofed coach type with them. The relevant diagram was E78 and they were built in 1905.

121. 'Star' class No. 4054 stands at Platform 4 of Newton Abbot station with an 'up' express. *Princess Charlotte* was completed in June 1914 and still had not been fitted with outside steam-pipes, these being added when the cylinders were replaced in October 1945. The gentleman on the left in plus-fours seems very interested in Mr. Soole taking the photograph.

122. Bristol Temple Meads station with the famous locomotive No. 6000 *King George V* awaiting departure from Platform 9 with an 'up' train. No. 6000 carries a local passenger code but this may be awaiting changing, the train having worked forward as an 'all stations' to Bristol. The train boards read 'Paddington-Bristol-Taunton' and of course should have been reversed for the return journey. Building work is in progress on the station, the whole layout being changed. Colour light signals have been installed in the centre but are not yet in use. Note the man standing on the windowsill of Bristol East signal box.

123. The men on the platform appear to be discussing No. 5027 *Farleigh Castle* whilst the young fireman watches Mr. Soole. Could it be that the driver has a small problem and has called for assistance from the shed? A '45XX' small prairie stands in one of the local platforms with a 'B'-set.

124. 'Hall' class No. 5962 *Wantage Hall* leaves Stoke Gifford behind as it heads towards Filton Junction and Bristol. Mr. Soole's records state this is a Wolverhampton-Penzance express, but as the first portion of the train is a mixture of Southern Railway vehicles, with a few GW types at the rear, this seems unlikely. Unless the train has come via Oxford its direction is also wrong. Once again the loco crew are watching Mr. Soole record them for posterity.

125. Here we see another running-in turn at Stapleton Road. This time the locomotive is No. 6018 *King Henry VI* which is in charge of a 'B'-set, each vehicle being to diagram E116. The station name board on the right is interesting for its two additions. One is presumably to help those who did not know where Stapleton Road was and above this is an advert for the Daily Mirror which states it is 'sold all along the line'. The pipe in the foreground is a mains water supply which crosses the girders of the bridge over St. Mark's Road.

126. A magnificent photograph showing a parcels train approaching the summit at Patchway, the end of the 5 miles of climbing from the Severn Tunnel. 'Bulldog' class 4—4—0 No. 3411 *Stanley Baldwin* seems to be making light work of the ascent, even with 18 vans and coaches behind the tender. This engine was built in April 1906, being nameless at first and numbered 3701. It was named in January 1909 and re-numbered in 1912. Its nameplates were subsequently removed in July 1937 (about 12 months after we see it here) the engine remaining nameless until withdrawal. The vehicles in the train include five Siphon 'G' vans, one an inside-framed version, another, the leading vehicle, is electrically lit. Seven GW passenger brake vans can also be seen, four of these being Dean 40′ vehicles, the others Collett designs, two of which are painted brown. The rest of the train is made-up of various examples of 4-wheeled vans. A shirt-sleeved track gang watch as the train passes by, the impression of a hot day further heightened by the lack of exhaust from the engine. A couple of vehicles are to be seen on the road to the station, along which the two gentlemen are strolling.

127. No. 4082 *Windsor Castle* leaves Westbury with a 'down' express under a fine signal gantry. This engine carries a plaque, seen on the cabside below the window, which commemorated King George V and Queen Mary driving the engine from Swindon Works to the station. *Windsor Castle* was always considered the 'Royal' engine to the extent that in 1952 it exchanged identities with No. 7013 *Bristol Castle* as it was unserviceable when required for the funeral of King George VI. In the foreground is a double compound point more commonly known as a double slip outside of the GWR. On the left may be seen a private-owner coal wagon of Dunkerton, Coal Factors, Bath.

128. This photograph is taken near Twyford and shows the four-track main line into London. Captured in this view is 4–6–0 No. 4089 *Donnington Castle* at the head of a 'down' express and it is running on the 'down' main line. No. 4089 was built in July 1925 and has had several modifications carried out, viz. whistle shield fitted, lamp bracket transferred to the smoke box door, and 4000 gallon tender in place of the 3500 gallon type. This locomotive had run a few years previously in an experimental lighter green. Note the mixture of vehicle ages and types in the train, ranging from clerestory to stock which was nearly new.

129. Rounding the curve from Patchway to Stoke Gifford is a parcels train from South Wales. The train is headed by *Viscount Churchill* which was rebuilt from the *Great Bear* and still carried that locomotive's number 111. Its driver is looking ahead at the junction signals. The first nine vehicles are all LNER stock, mainly fish vans but including an ex-NER example and a fruit van. Following behind these are a GWR passenger brake van and an inside-framed 'Monster' — a 50' scenery van — with some empty carriages next. On the embankment, in front of the signal, is a fogman's hut, used when the weather or a failure dictated. The fogman's duty was to place detonators on the track to prevent or warn a driver not to pass a signal at danger.

130. With Westbury station to the rear, 4—6—0 No. 6019 *King Henry V* heads the 3.30 p.m. Paddington-Penzance express westward. No. 6019 will head the train as far as its home shed at Plymouth, where it will come off, the train carrying on to Penzance. 'King' class locomotives were prohibited from crossing the Royal Albert bridge at Saltash.

131. A Paddington-Bristol-Weston-Super-Mare express leaves Bristol and is passing under Bath Road bridge on its journey west. The train is headed by 'Castle' class 4—6—0 No. 5084 *Reading Abbey*. This locomotive was rebuilt from 'Star' class No. 4064 which carried the same name. Coaching stock on the train includes brake third No. 5365 completed in 1930 to diagram D111 on Lot 1448, followed by one of the early Collett composites which were fitted with 9′ 0″ 'fishbelly' bogies. Behind these two is a 'dreadnought' dining car, so called because they were built at the same time as the famous battleship and were of massive proportion.

132. A 'down' express thunders under an overbridge on the Frome avoiding line. The visible part of the train is composed of 'centenary' stock. No. 6004 *King George III*, at the head, is a Laira locomotive and is working home. This line was opened in 1933 and is therefore fairly new. It was constructed to allow a shorter journey to the West Country.

Appendix

Within this work we have included the most commonly used reference system for stock. Whilst easily recognised by most enthusiasts, particularly those who have studied Swindon products, others may be confused. In the bibliography at the end of this appendix further reading for those who wish to pursue a greater depth of knowledge can be found. It is perhaps helpful, however, to give an explanation here of the terms used in the captions and in the detailed lists of train formations in this appendix.

From about 1910 all GWR rolling stock was given a diagram number. This number was made-up of a letter which identified the type of vehicle and a number which identified the sub-type. The identification letters were allocated as follows for carriage and wagon stock.

CARRIAGE STOCK

A — First class coaches of all bogie types.
B — Allocated for second class but never issued.
C — Third class coaches of bogie type excluding those with a brake compartment.
D — Brake third class bogie coaches.
E — Composite first/third class bogie coaches of all types.
F — Slip coaches of all bogie types.
G — Saloons of all types.
H — Restaurant, kitchen, buffet and dining coaches, all bogie types.
J — Sleeping coaches, all bogie types.
K — Passenger Brake/Luggage Vans of bogie types (PBVs).
L — Travelling Post Office and Mail bag vans of bogie type.
M — Parcels and Newspaper vehicles of bogie type.
N — Horse Boxes (all 4-wheel).
O — Milk and Fish vehicles.
P — Carriage and Scenery vehicles both open and covered.
R — 4 or 6-wheeled first class coaches.
S — 4 or 6-wheeled third class excluding brake coaches.
T — 4 or 6-wheeled brake third class coaches.
U — 4 or 6-wheeled composite first/third class coaches.
V — 4 or 6-wheeled Passenger Brake Vans.
W — 4 or 6-wheeled vans not included under V, including Bullion, Parcels and Hounds Vans.

GOODS STOCK

A — Girder wagons.
B — Armour plate and roll wagons.
C — Boiler trucks and trolleys.
D — Glass wagons.
E — Wheel and propeller wagons.
F — Road roller trucks.
G — Flat, well and covered wagons for road vehicles.
H — Flat wagons, for aeroplane traffic, containers etc.
J — Rail and timber wagons.
K — Crane testing wagons.
L — Match trucks.
M — Shunting Trucks.
N — Loco coal and mineral wagons.
O — Open goods wagons.

P — Ballast wagons.
Q — Provender wagons.
R — Manure wagons.
S — Fish wagons.
T — Permanent way and sleeper wagons.
U — Stone wagons.
V — Covered goods and grain vans.
W — Cattle wagons.
X — Meat vans.
Y — Fruit and banana vans.
Z — Gunpowder vans.
AA — Brake vans.
BB — Stores vans.
CC — Workshop and tool vans.
DD — Tank wagons.
EE — Flat wagons for demountable tanks.
FF — Trestle plate wagons.

There were approximately thirty-six different telegraphic codes which were each sub-divided to identify different size and capacity of wagons. Also the carriage stock was identified in a similar way to simplify telegraphic requests. Of these names we have only used a few for the goods stock e.g. Toad for 'Goods' brake vans, Open for 'Open' goods wagons, Mink for 'Covered' goods vans. In the carriage stock it was used basically only for the non-passenger types, where we have used the codes which were in most cases carried on the vehicle sides e.g. Siphon for 'Milk/Fish' vans.

Most of the GWR coaching stock has been given semi-official type names by enthusiasts and historians, some from their introduction and some evolved over the subsequent years. These originated in various ways, the name 'clerestory' referring to the type of roof whereas 'toplight' refers to the windows above the main windows on the coach sides.

It is interesting to note in these photographs the evolution of the GWR coaches during this period. The introduction by G. J. Churchward of the 70 foot stock showed progression from a single clerestory type via the 'dreadnought', 'concertina' and 'toplight' types and culminated in the Collett vehicles. Then in the thirties, the near standard window sizes were phased out giving way to the larger windows seen in the 1935 and subsequent stock.

The pattern of one door on each side of a compartment was dispensed with in the 'dreadnought' stock but re-introduced, after public reaction, on the following 'concertina' type. This style continued into the Collett era until the 1935 stock, although some corridor side doors had been dispensed with a few years earlier.

For those photographs where other companies' stock is shown we have tried wherever possible to identify these. Within the LMS coaches in the make-up lists the more familiar British Rail code has been used in place of the less well-known LMS one. Also the ex-LNWR stock has been identified wherever possible.

A large number of private owner wagons were common in the thirties, but now alas are no more. These must have provided the observer and photographer with a moving atlas of place names. Some wagons have been highlighted but we will leave it to the reader to identify others.

We list below the coach types in chronological order, also the relevant diagram numbers are shown to assist in the reading of the train formation lists.

Clerestory

In this case we have only quoted the diagrams of the vehicles seen in the photographs and those which appear similar.

NON GANGWAYED — C3, 10, 14.
E25, E39, E45, E72.

GANGWAYED — C17, 18.
D30/72/73.
E65, 69.

Dreadnought — 69′/70′ x 9′ 6″ all gangwayed.
C24; D42; H8-11.

Concertina — 70′ x 9′ all gangwayed.
C27; D43; E79, 80, 81; H13-15.

Toplight — 56′/57′/70′ x 9′ — only gangwayed quoted.
This type of coach was sub-divided into a number of types:—

BARS 1 — Bar truss underframe, horizontal eave panels and single toplight above end corridor windows.
56′ — C30; E82.
57′ — C31; D44, 45, 47, 68, 80; E83, 88.
70′ — C29; D48.

BARS 2 — Bar truss underframe, panels alongside windows go up to cantrail and double toplights above end corridor windows.
57′ — C31; D47; E88, 94, 95.
70′ — C29; D51; E93.

MULTIBAR — Twin rod truss underframe, same bodies as BARS 2, others steel panelled.
57′ — C31; D56, 88.
70′ — C29, 33; D57, 69; E99, 102, 104.

ANGLE TRUSS — Angle truss underframe and steel panelled bodies.
57′ — C32, 35; D56.
70′ — D69; E99, 102, 104.

RESTAURANT VEHICLES

H16 — 21, 24.

Collett — 1922 — 70′ x 9′ all gangwayed.
C44, 45, 46, 50; D82, 83, 84, 90; E109, 110, 111, 112; H26, 27, 28, 29.

Collett — 1923 — 57′ x 9′ all gangwayed.
C54, 57; D94, 95; E114, 115, 118, 127, 128, 132; H25, 33.

Collett — 1928 — 57′ x 8′ 10¼″ all gangwayed.
C58; D104.

Collett — 1929 — Riviera Stock — 60′ x 9′ 5¾″
C59; D105, 106, 108; E137, 138; H35-37.

Collett — 1929 — 60′ x 9′
C60; E139; H38.

Collett — 1930 — 60′ x 9′ 3″.
C62; D111, 115.

Collett — 1932 — 60′ x 9′ 3″.
C64; H39, 40.

Collett — 1933 — 57′ x 9′.
C67; D116, 118; E146, 148; H41.

Collett — 1934/5 — Centenary
C69; D120; E149, 150; H43, 44.

Collett — 1935-1938 — 'Modern'
A20; C70, 73, 77; D121, 124; E151-155, 158-160.

Note not all of the restaurant vehicles are quoted above as they were contemporary with, but not built in such easily defined periods and sizes, as the standard stock.

NON-CORRIDOR — 'B'-SETS

These comprised a pair of brake composite coaches coupled with the brake compartments at the outer ends; some sets were permanently close-coupled.

1923 — E116 x 2; 1925 — E129 x 2; 1929 — E140 x 2.
1932 — E145 x 2; 1933 — E147 x 2.

Train Formations

The lists below give the identities where possible of the locomotives and rolling stock in the trains and in the foreground/background. Where we find difficulty differentiating between the various similar coach designs, which were externally identical to others but had an internal or minor alteration, we have placed the + sign. Swindon, on such occasions, issued another diagram. In these instances we have shown the first of the possible diagrams.

1. No. 4987 *Brockley Hall* built 1/31, withdrawn 4/62.
   LMS ex-LNW dia. 268 TK, LMS ex-LNWR BTK, LMS, LMS, etc.

2. No. 6016 *King Edward V* built 6/28, withdrawn 9/62.
   C67, C54+, D48, E102.

3. No. 4075 *Cardiff Castle* built 1/24, withdrawn 11/61.
   P15, C14, D95+, E —.

4. No. 4061 *Glastonbury Abbey* built 5/22, withdrawn 3/57.
   D105, C54+, C54+.

5. No. 5048 *Cranbrook Castle* built 4/36, withdrawn 8/62.
   N13. Beyond, LMS TK dia. 1899 No. 1936, Lot 896.

6. No. 5046 *Clifford Castle* built 4/36, withdrawn 9/62.
   E99+, C31, E128, H26+, D88, C33, C31/2, D121, E151, C70, D121, —.

7. No. 3176 built 11/07, withdrawn 11/57.
   AA4, AA18, Tredegar No. 3874, Renwick-Wilton, GLM, Baldwin, —.

8. No. 5212 built 10/23, withdrawn 5/62.
   Marcroft Wagons, Swansea No. 442.

9. No. 6002 *King William IV* built 7/27, withdrawn 9/62.
   C30+, C30+, —.

10. No. 2526 built 5/1897, withdrawn 10/40.
    E147, E147 (B-set).

11. No. 4035 *Queen Charlotte* built 11/10, withdrawn 10/51.
    D106, C59, E137, H8+, —.

12. No. 6025 *King Henry III* built 7/30, withdrawn 12/62.
    C10, K14+, G20, G20, C10, C10.

13. No. 6029 *King Edward VIII* built 8/30, withdrawn 7/62.
    D121, C70, E151, H41, E151, C70, D121.
14. No. 4064 *Reading Abbey* built 12/22, withdrawn 4/37 (rebuilt).
    D95+, C54+, E127+, H8/11, — .
15. No. 5565 built 1/29, withdrawn 9/60.
    E140/145, E140/145 (B-set).
16. No. 5554 built 11/28, withdrawn 8/63.
    C60, C54, E82, C18.
17. '54XX'.
    A26, C60.
18. No. 4354 built 3/14, withdrawn 2/39.
    E80, C3, C10, C10, C79, C54+, C32, — .
19. No. 2243 built 6/12, withdrawn 12/34.
    D49, E89, E89, D49, K—, — .
20. No. 6339 built 6/21, withdrawn 7/62.
    L9, — .
21. No. 5022 *Wigmore Castle* built 8/32, withdrawn 6/63.
    D118, C67, E127+, D118, — .
22. No. 6024 *King Edward I* built 6/30, withdrawn 6/62 (preserved).
    D42, H25/33, C27, E81, D82+, E109+.
23. No. 4094 *Dynevor Castle* built 5/26, withdrawn 3/62.
    D95+, E127+.
24. No. 6029 *King Stephen* built 8/30, withdrawn 6/62.
    D42, H25/33, C27, E81, D82+.
25. No. 5043 *Barbury Castle* built 3/36, withdrawn 12/63 (preserved).
    H17/18, H15, — .
26. No. 2949 *Stanford Court* built 5/12, withdrawn 1/52.
    D108, — .
27. No. 3731 built 7/37, withdrawn 5/64.
    M1 No. 41867.
28. No. 2812 built 11/05, withdrawn 1/59.
29. No. 4061 *Glastonbury Abbey* built 5/22, withdrawn 3/57.
    SR ex-LBSCR milk van, LMS dia. 1720 BCK, D52, LMS dia. 1743 diner, E127+, — .
30. No. 6014 *King Henry VII* built 5/28, withdrawn 9/62.
    D44, C60+, — .
31. No. 4098 *Kidwelly Castle* built 7/26, withdrawn 12/63.
    E128, D95+, E127+, D118, LMS 12-wheel diner, — .
32. No. 4055 *Princess Sophia* built 7/14, withdrawn 2/51.
    C32/35, D30, SR, SR, SR.
33. No. 3396 *Natal Colony* built 1/04, withdrawn 3/48.
    E140, E140 (B-set).
34. No. 5118 built 12/05, rebuilt 5/28, withdrawn 3/38.
    Baldwin, Baldwin, Baldwin, Baldwin, O16/9, GLM No. 30275, — .
35. No. 3174 built 10/07, withdrawn 3/58. No. 5243 built 8/24, withdrawn 11/64.
    J. Snow & Co. No. 417, T. T. Pascoe No. 259, ?, ?, ?, ?, Tredegar, Camroux, — .
36. '3150' class & '28XX' class.
37. No. 4043 *Prince Henry* built 5/13, withdrawn 1/52.
    G18, K38, C33, C31, D95+, E127+, LMS 12-wheel diner, — .
38. No. 4349 built 2/14, withdrawn 6/38.
    O11, D115, E139+, E127+, C54+, D94.
39. No. 6028 *King George VI* built 7/30, withdrawn 11/62.
    D69, C44+, E109, D43, — .
40. No. 6027 *King Richard I* built 7/30, withdrawn 9/62.
    D69 No. 3795.
41. Bristol Temple Meads.
42. Bristol Temple Meads north end.
    C29, D121, E115/8, C70, at platform.
43. Bristol Temple Meads.
44. Dr. Day's carriage sidings — mixed stock.
45. Bristol West.
    O5, L22 with various companies' vehicles behind.
46. Bristol Temple Meads.
47. Bristol Temple Meads.
48. Bristol Temple Meads.
49. No. 4037 *The South Wales Borderers* built 12/10, rebuilt 6/26, withdrawn 9/62.
50. No. 5032 *Usk Castle* built 5/34, withdrawn 9/62.
    Tender No. 2586 built 8/31, withdrawn 11/63.
51. No. 111 *Viscount Churchill* built 9/24, (ex-*Great Bear*) withdrawn 7/53.
52. No. 6027 *King Richard I* built 7/30, withdrawn 9/62.
    C59. C70, E150, E150, D120, E149, H47, H48, C69, C69, D120, E150, E148.
53. No. 4095 *Harlech Castle* built 6/26, withdrawn 12/62.
    D104, E139+, C67, D42, — .
54. No. 4092 *Dunraven Castle* built 8/25, withdrawn 12/61.
    D118, E88, C54+, D95+, C67, — .
55. No. 4033 *Queen Victoria* built 11/10, withdrawn 6/51.
    O11, D45, E139+, H8+, — .
56. No. 4091 *Dudley Castle* built 7/25, withdrawn 1/59. '28XX'.
    C62, C54+, C54+, D43, — .
57. No. 5005 *Manorbier Castle* built 6/27, withdrawn 2/60.
    H17, H16, — .
58. No. 5010 *Restormel Castle* built 7/27, withdrawn 10/59.
    G33, C54+, C32, C17, C54, — .
59. No. 4025 *Italian Monarch* built 7/09, withdrawn 8/50.
    E148, E148, D95+, E88, D—, — .
60. No. 6015 *King Richard III* built 6/28, withdrawn 9/62.
    D118, C67, H15, E88, D80, E138, E99+, E128.
61. No. 4028 *Roumanian Monarch* built 9/09, withdrawn 11/51.
    C32, LMS, D94, E127+, LMS, LMS, LMS, — .
62. No. 4064 *Reading Abbey* built 12/22, withdrawn 2/37 (rebuilt).
    D95+, C54+, E127+, H8/11, E88, D95+, E—, E99+, G60/1.
63. No. 5029 *Nunney Castle* built 5/34 withdrawn 12/63 (preserved).
    C.32, D121, H15, — .
64. No. 5031 *Totnes Castle* built 5/34, withdrawn 10/63.
    D47, E88, H13/14, C67, D—, — .
65. No. 4068 *Llanthony Abbey* built 1/23, withdrawn 9/62.
    SR ex-LSWR milk van, K38, K38, — .
66. No. 5034 *Corfe Castle* built 5/35, withdrawn 9/62.
    E94, D95+, E127+, H38, D45+, E127+, D118, D118, D95+.
67. No. 5010 *Restormel Castle* built 7/27, withdrawn 10/59.
    E113, C30, C54+, C59, —

68. No. 5013 *Abergavenny Castle* built 6/32, withdrawn 7/62.
C54 No. 5196, C59.
69. No. 3176 built 11/07, withdrawn 11/57. No. 3392 *New Zealand* built 1/04, withdrawn 1/37.
LNER vans, − .
70. No. 557 built 11/28, withdrawn 10/60.
C32, E128, − . Beyond, A13.
71. No. 1163 built 3/1876, withdrawn 5/46.
E45, C10.
72. No. 1 built 12/33, withdrawn 8/55.
73. No. 6820 *Kingstone Grange* built 1/37, withdrawn 7/65.
Camroux No. 23, WAC, AAC Anthracite, Bedwas, − .
74. No. 2902 *Lady of the Lake* built 5/06, withdrawn 8/49.
O33, − , ex-TVR, − .
75. No. 4377 built 12/15, withdrawn 1/59.
Llanbradnach (Cardiff Coll. Ltd.) No. 1262.
76. No. 6014 *King Henry VII* built 5/28, withdrawn 9/62.
D121, C70, E151, H41, E151, E151, D121.
77. No. 6009 *King Charles II* built 3/28, withdrawn 9/62.
D106, E155, C77, C54+, − .
78. No. 4022 *Belgian Monarch* built 6/09, withdrawn 2/52.
E128, H38, E146, − .
79. No. 5039 *Rhuddlan Castle* built 6/35, withdrawn 6/64.
K40, C32, C60/62, E88, H13, − .
80. No. 4020 *Knight Commander* built 5/08, withdrawn 3/51.
D95, C59, E127+, D56, D118, C54+, E69+, D118.
81. No. 5056 *Ogmore Castle* built 6/36, withdrawn 11/64.
LMS period III TO, C54+, LMS ex-LNWR dia. 213 BCK, O33, LMS ex-LNWR B− , − .
82. No. 4999 *Gopsal Hall* built 3/31, withdrawn 9/62.
N11, E83, D45+, E127+, H38, D95+, E127+, D95+, C70, D118, E− .
83. No. 4044 *Prince George* built 5/13, withdrawn 2/53.
SR, SR, SR, SR, SR, O11.
84. No. 6027 *King Richard I* built 7/30, withdrawn 9/62.
85. No. 6014 *King Henry VII* built 5/28, withdrawn 9/62.
C29, C44+, E109+, H8+, − .
86. No. 5013 *Abergavenny Castle* built 7/62.
D43, C44+, E109+, D83/90, H8+, E152/3, E93, − .
87. No. 5044 *Beverston Castle* built 3/36, withdrawn 4/62.
D94, C54+, E127+, − .
88. No. 5036 *Lyonshall Castle* built 5/35, withdrawn 9/62.
D121, C73, E154, H41, E−, C73, D124.
89. No. 4038 *Queen Berengaria* built 1/11, withdrawn 4/52.
LNER ex-GCR stock.
90. No. 5011 *Tintagel Castle* built 7/27, withdrawn 9/62.
C18, D68, E65+, D95+, C73/77, − .
91. No. 5062 *Earl of Shaftesbury* built 6/37, withdrawn 8/62.
N16, LMS, LMS ex-LNWR dia. 446, E95, D94, E127+, D108+, H16.
92. No. 4082 *Windsor Castle* built 4/24, withdrawn 9/64.
LMS ex-LNWR Royal train − BFK dia. 127A No. 5154/5, Royal Saloon, − .

93. No. 6027 *King Richard I* built 7/30, withdrawn 9/62.
D94, C54+.
94. No. 4945 *Milligan Hall* built 8/29, withdrawn 11/61.
N12/13.
95. No. 6003 *King George IV* built 7/27, withdrawn 6/62.
D121, C70, E151, H41, E151, − .
96. No. 2987 *Bride of Lammermoor* built 8/05, withdrawn 10/49.
D72/73, E93, C54+, D116, K14+, − .
97. No. 5224 built 5/24, withdrawn 5/64.
E72, E25.
98. No. 5002 *Ludlow Castle* built 9/26, withdrawn 9/64.
E152, H26+, D45+, C70, C54+, C67, D121, E154, C70, D121, D82, − .
99. No. 5053 *Bishop's Castle* built 5/36, withdrawn 7/62.
LMS ex-LNWR dia. 208 BCK, LMS ex-MR, LMS ex-LNWR BTK, − .
100. No. 5040 *Stokesay Castle* built 6/35, withdrawn 10/63.
D121, C73, E155, H41, E154, C73, D121, C44+, − .
101. No. 5245 built 11/25, withdrawn 10/64.
LNER van, SR 9-plank, LMS 3-plank, LMS 3-plank, − .
102. No. 2810 built 10/05, withdrawn 9/59.
WAC, − , AAC Anthracite, − .
103. No. 3376 *River Plym* built 5/03, withdrawn 9/48.
E39, C43, C4, C3/10, − .
104. No. 4096 *Highclere Castle* built 6/26, withdrawn 1/63.
K29, C67, D104, E115/118, H38, − .
105. No. 5040 *Stokesay Castle* built 6/35, withdrawn 10/63.
H17/18, H15, E137, D43, E79/81, D111, D43, E109+, M14.
106. No. 6000 *King George V* built 6/27, withdrawn 12/62 (preserved).
107. '4575' class.
E129, E129 (B-set), C3.
108. No. 6024 *King Edward I* built 6/30, withdrawn 6/62 (preserved).
C77, C73, C54+, C67, − .
109. No. 6009 *King Charles II* built 3/28, withdrawn 9/62.
C58.
110. No. 5028 *Llantilo Castle* built 5/34, withdrawn 5/60.
E95, D94, E115/8, D95+, − .
111. No. 5027 *Farleigh Castle* built 4/34, withdrawn 11/62.
D121, C73, E158, H41, A20, C73/7, D121.
112. No. 5047 *Compton Castle* built 4/36, withdrawn 9/62.
H17, H24, E139+, C54, C62, D51, − .
113. No. 4075 *Cardiff Castle* built 1/24, withdrawn 11/61.
D121, H24, E139+, C54+, D51, − .
114. No. 4926 *Fairleigh Hall* built 5/29, withdrawn 9/61.
E140, E140 (B-set).
115. No. 6025 *King Henry III* built 7/30, withdrawn 12/62.
H35, H36/37, H45, D57/69, H11, D43, C−, C−, E110+.
116. No. 4094 *Dynevor Castle* built 5/26, withdrawn 3/62.
L22, C27, E152, O11, LMS, − .
117. No. 4055 *Princess Sophia* built 7/14, withdrawn 2/51.
E128, − .

118. No. 3159 built 5/07, withdrawn 11/49. '28XX' class.

119. No. 2819 built 12/05, withdrawn 1/61.
O5, O2/3, O5, O4, O5, O5, O4, O5, O5, O4, O5, — .

120. No. 4932 *Evenley Hall* built 6/29, withdrawn 11/64.
E78, H13/4, E152/3, D121, E127+, D121, LMS, D105, — .

121. No. 4054 *Princess Charlotte* built 6/14, withdrawn 2/52.
C29, — .

122. No. 6000 *King George V* built 6/27, withdrawn 12/62 (preserved).
D88, E127+, C32, C54+.

123. No. 5027 *Farleigh Castle* built 4/34, withdrawn 11/62.
C54+, C54+, D95+.

124. No. 5962 *Wantage Hall* built 7/36, withdrawn 11/64.
SR stock.

125. No. 6018 *King Henry VI* built 6/28, withdrawn 12/62.
E116, E116 (B-set).

126. No. 3411 *Stanley Baldwin* built 4/06, withdrawn 10/38.
O11, K29/30, LNER van, LNER van, LNER van, LNER van, LNER van, K42, O11, S8, O11, K42, O22, K14, K14, K29/30, O11, K41.

127. No. 4082 *Windsor Castle* built 4/24, withdrawn 9/64.
C58, H40, H39, — .

128. No. 4089 *Donnington Castle* built 7/25, withdrawn 9/64.
O11, E137, H— , D121, C20, D121, C70, E151, E151, D121, C24, — .

129 No. 111 *Viscount Churchill* built 9/24 (ex-*Great Bear*), withdrawn 7/53.
LNER fish vans, — .

130. No. 6019 *King Henry V* built 7/28, withdrawn 9/62.
D69, C44, E109+, D43, H15, — .

131. No. 5084 *Reading Abbey* built 12/22, rebuilt 4/37, withdrawn 7/62.
D111, E115/8, H8+, — .

132. No. 6004 *King George III* built 7/27, withdrawn 6/62.
D120, E149, — .

This photograph shows 'Castle' class 4—6—0 No. 4016 *Knight of the Golden Fleece*, which was built as a 'Star' class in 1908 and converted to a 'Castle' in 1925. The locomotive is just starting away from Bristol Temple Meads with an 'up' express. Note the mud hole cover fairing next to the cab is not screwed in its correct position. In the left foreground members of the public and a railway worker stand on the boardwalk waiting to cross. The use by the public of this was probably a result of the rebuilding which took place at Temple Meads in 1935.

Additional Information and Corrections

A number of errors have come to light following production of the first edition, some due to ignorance, some to transcription but all down to us. Of these, a few have been pointed out to us by others to whom we are extremely grateful. We have also taken the opportunity to include some of the information recently available to us where it applies to those photographs already published.

Photo 1.
> Parsons Street should be Parson Street. Taken on Sunday 23rd of July 1933 of a Torquay & Paignton – Liverpool express.

Photo 7.
> Taken at 2.05 p.m. on Wednesday, the 5th of April 1933.

Photo 8.
> A Bristol – South Wales empties restarts after having the brakes pinned down, on the 14th of August 1933 at 12.12p.m.

Photo 9.
> The 'up' 9.55a.m. from Ilfracombe at 2.00p.m. June 26th 1922.

Photo 11.
> The wagon named Portwell, etc., is in fact Whitwell, Cole & Co. of Bristol. The engine is No. 4039 *Queen Matilda* on 5.15 p.m. two hour express at 5.20 p.m. 25th of July 1933.

Photo 12.
> Taken at 3.04 p.m. on the 8th of August 1933.

Photo 15.
> Timed at 2.46 p.m. on August 22nd 1933, this view was recorded some 29 minutes after that in Photo 103.

Photo 28.
> Seen on Saturday, August 19th 1933 at 1.40 p.m.

Photo 29.
> Mr. Soole named this as a Wolverhampton train, but it may be a west to north. The caption is misleading as we said it was a Wolverhampton train running via the Severn Tunnel when of course these trains ran via the LMS line to Standish Junction. The train has the appearance of the 1.00 p.m. Plymouth – Crewe which would pass this location at approx. 4.20 p.m. However, the order of the coaches doesn't fit any known pattern and the train is on the 'up'

main line, although it could change over at Filton Junction. The engine is from Bristol, so is of no assistance in identifying this train.

Photo 39.
> The wagon belongs to Snow of Glastonbury, not Shaw.

Photo 46.
> It should read 'to Redcliffe goods', not Redlands which is on the Clifton line.

Photo 55.
> The records state this to be a Brighton – Cardiff train but one of the coaches, the Dreadnought, wouldn't be allowed over this route, so unless added elsewhere, this couldn't be a train from Brighton.

Photo 61.
> Recorded as the northbound Devonian on August 19th 1933.

Photo 79.
> Tool van No. 31 wasn't a Bristol Van, this is in fact Tool van No. 91.

Photo 97
> A Filton – Bristol local on the 12th of August 1933.

Photo 103.
> Snyed Park should read Sneyd Park.

Photo 124.
> This caption created more comment than any other. The train is what we stated originally, not a Wolverhampton to Penzance. The headcode is that of an 'up' express from South Wales, so is entirely wrong. After the war this code was used as that quoted by Mr. Soole, which may have caused the confusion. It might be a special, but it isn't a scheduled train. We have never found a true listing for these headcodes despite a long search, but most of those that we see fall into the known pattern of the period.

Photo in appendices.
> Taken on Easter Tuesday showing the 'up' 11.45 a.m. setting off. In the background is a LMS Derby & Birmingham – Bristol express just arriving. Dated April 18th 1933.

Bibliography

RCTS Locos of the GWR – RCTS. Parts 1-12.
Stars, Castle and Kings – Nock – D & C Prts 1 and 2.
Standard gauge 4-4-0s – Nock – D & C Parts 1 and 2.
A History of GWR Goods Wagons – Atkins, Beard, Hyde & Tourret. D & C Parts 1 and 2.
A Pictorial Record of GW Coaches – Rusell – OPC Parts 1 and 2 plus Appendix.
A Pictorial Record of GW Wagons – Russell – OPC and Appendix.
An Illustrated History of LMS Coaches – Jenkinson & Essery – OPC.
An Illustrated History of LMS Wagons – Essery – OPC.
Great Western Signalling – Vaughan – OPC.
Castle & Kings at Work – Rutherford – Ian Allan.
Great Western Way – Slinn – HMRS.
Track Diagrams of the GWR – Cooke.
Great Western Coaches 1890-1954 – Harris – D & C.

Acknowledgements

We would like to acknowledge the assistance given to us by the following:- Mrs Marjorie D Soole, the staff of the NRM library at York, members of the Great Western Group (NE Area), Paul Karau, Dave Cross and Keith Ettle of Bristol, Dave Clark and Owen Lancaster for assistance on other company stock. In addition, Leslie, Margaret and Sue for typing and lastly our wives and families for their great patience.